The New You
REVOLUTION™

A 40 Day Journey to Discovering and Becoming the New You

Latoya A. Benson

The New You Revolution
A 40 Day Journey to Discovering and Becoming the New You

Unless otherwise noted, all scripture quotations are taken from the King James Version of the Bible.

Scripture quotations marked AMP are taken from the Amplified® Bible, Copyright © 1954, 1958, 1962, 1964, 1965, 1987 by The Lockman Foundation. Used by permission.

Scripture quotations marked NLT are taken from the Holy Bible, New Living Translation, copyright © 1996, 2004, 2007 by Tyndale House Foundation. Used by permission of Tyndale House Publishers, Inc., Carol Stream, Illinois 60188. All rights reserved.

Scripture quotations marked NIV are taken from the THE HOLY BIBLE, NEW INTERNATIONAL VERSION®, NIV® Copyright © 1973, 1978, 1984, 2011 by Biblica, Inc.® Used by permission. All rights reserved worldwide.

Scripture quotations marked MSG are taken from The Message Bible. Copyright © 1993, 1994, 1995, 1996, 2000, 2001, 2002. Used by permission of NavPress Publishing Group. Used by permission.

ISBN-13: 978-0692255131

Printed in the United States of America

For information regarding discounts for bulk orders, please contact The New You Revolution at thenewyourevolution@gmail.com

ACKNOWLEDGEMENTS

As I sit and reflect on the thought that I am now an author, I am filled with gratitude and praise to God. I love God and I give Him all the glory and honor. My one desire is to fulfill the purpose for which He has sent me. I am overwhelmed by the love and support of my entire family. I thank you all for believing in me even when you didn't understand my decisions. I want to express my sincere and deepest love to my mother Sheila A. Benson. Thank you for your unselfish love, your sacrifice, your listening ear and your support. I am especially grateful for your time and attention to editing my first book. I pray that this is the launching pad to your successful future in editing. To my father, Marion A. McClain, I thank you for your sound advice and wisdom that assisted me in making some very tough decisions. Your love towards me does not go unnoticed. I am extremely proud to say that I am a mother of two. I am excited that Malachi and Maysa have a tangible representation of what faith, focus, and hard work can produce. I declare that you both will grow up to do greater than what I have done. I want to give a special shout out to my amazing friends who keep me grounded, make me laugh, and encourage me along the way. Tanea, Tasha, JeNeal, Michele, Nemahun, and Shalethia…you ladies are the best! A special thank you to my wonder twin who has empowered me and challenged me to open my mind and embrace that which I couldn't see. There are some people who you instantly connect with and you realize that it is for sure a God connection. To my west coast sister Charlene Feathers, I am so grateful for your friendship and I will never forget your sacrifice and time as I transformed into a new woman. To Veronica, thank you for your prayers and willingness to be there for me no matter what. And of course, I want to thank my glam squad Bree Auree – Wardrobe Stylist and Sharonda Sullivan – Make-up Artist for assisting in creating my look for the book cover just like I envisioned it. Also a special thank you to fashion photographer Rodney Young. I am more than grateful to EVERYONE who has been a blessing to my life. You are appreciated.

CONTENTS

Celebrate Yourself!

Celebrate Yourself!

Celebrate Yourself!

iv

THE INTRODUCTION

The Journey

I am so ecstatic that you have chosen to embark on this 40 day journey. I truly believe your life will be enriched and you will experience a shift in your mind that will lead to a lifestyle change and, ultimately, a transformation. This spiritual guide is birthed out of my own experience. All God needed was for me to give Him 40 days; 40 days of surrender, honesty, focus, prayer, fasting, and communication. Sounds simple right? Well, it wasn't exactly an easy pill for me to swallow. Although I was already in a place of transition by circumstance, God was thrusting me into a spiritual transition and a shift in my mind. I want to take a moment and share with you a portion of my journey.

I remember growing up knowing that I was different and that God's hand was on my life. At a very young age, I began searching for my identity but, never being able to embody it. I wanted desperately to connect with something or someone that looked like me. When I looked in the mirror I saw the obvious, the outward appearance, but I needed to know the girl behind the shell. My struggle was never external, but it was an internal tug of war. Am I pretty enough? Why don't they like me? Do I have what it takes? These were just a few questions that often ran through my mind. I longed for the loneliness to cease and the void to be filled. God often sent visions and dreams to show me what I possessed inside, but I struggled to believe it. I knew there was something extraordinary on the inside of me, but I struggled to become it.

So as a teenage girl, I sought to connect myself with people and relationships that I thought would complete me and make me whole. Instead, I constantly came up emotionally bankrupt. Rather than deal with my issues and face them head on, I continued operating in the same behaviors which produced the same results. At the age of sixteen, I dealt with a major life-changing situation. Because of mistakes and bad decisions, I suffered with an overwhelming amount of guilt and self-condemnation. I fell into a deep depression. I was so angry at myself for not making smarter decisions. I was angry at God because I felt like I made one mistake and He punished me for it, but I understood later that this was another opportunity for me to grow and let God fix my life. But I did like always, cried out to God, swept it under the rug, I managed the hurt and pain, and kept it moving. I knew God was my answer, but I didn't know how to let Him in. Yes, I always prayed. Yes, I knew God but, to my surprise, it was all on the surface. After all, my father wasn't actively in my life so I didn't know how to let another man in and receive love. Every time I let someone in, they hurt or rejected me so, subconsciously, I placed a huge wall in front of the doorway to my heart. As a result, I treated God the same way not realizing that He was nothing like the other men in my life. He was my father and He wanted to love me, show me how to love, and make me new. As time went on, my relationship with God continued to grow. I was growing stronger, evolving as a woman and I even got married. Yes, marriage was my dream because I knew that I was designed to be a wife. I married at the age of 26 and instantly became a part of a ready-made family. I was tough, independent, mature, and strong, so I was ready to handle it all. However, I didn't realize how difficult it would be managing my role as a wife, mother, and the "me" issues. But I loved being married and was committed to it just as I was committed to God, but there was still that one area in my relationship with God that was off limits. You know how we do ladies, we may share some things but this right here, is OFF LIMITS. I knew God wanted to process me

4

but I never wanted to take time and put in the necessary sacrifices and work to be delivered from my bad habits, strongholds, hurt, and pain. So I became comfortable with getting quick fixes instead of allowing God to take me through the process. I would start the process but somehow work my way out of it when it came too close to those deep-seeded issues. This behavior would allow me to walk in seasonal manifested blessings and see glimpses of the "good life" but always stopping short of the fullness of what God had for me. I knew that what God had for me was far beyond what I had ever experienced and I also knew that there was a set time for me to go through a metamorphosis. It probably wouldn't be the most comfortable experience but, I knew afterwards, I would be free and able to walk in my purpose! Well sure enough the time had come.

In 2011, I went through a major transition. After six years my husband and I separated and I began my journey of separation and divorce. It rocked my very foundation! How did this happen? Where did I go wrong? This was not the life I imagined. Did some spirit come in and bamboozle me? God, I need answers. It was as if I was experiencing the worst time of my life yet, in some unexplainable way, I understood that this was my appointed time. All those other trials were just preparing me for what was to come. It was time for me to have an encounter with God that I had never experienced; one that would change my life forever. Can you say scared.com? Yes, I had been processed through other things. Yes, God anointed me for a great work, but this time it was different. There was a different weight to the oil God was pouring.

I remember lying in bed so broken and I was crying out to God. I heard the Lord clearly say, "Just give me 40 days." I knew those 40 days would be a defining moment in my life; that I would be shifted in my mind and my spirit. I knew that I would be whole and healed. But even knowing that, those old feelings of fear appeared and it took me a while to be obedient and surrender unto God completely. God spoke to me and told me that He would teach me how to reinvent myself. This transition I was experiencing would be the vehicle to transform me into the new person God already called me to be. Just like there was a set time for me, there is a set time for you. It is time that you have a unique encounter with God to become the new you.

The New You Revolution – A 40 Day Journey to Discovering and Becoming the New You is a proclamation that it is time to relaunch. God said that just like a car is recalled to repair faulty parts, and defects or to release an updated version, the same process needs to take place with you. Alone time with God is necessary for spiritual cleansing of habits, thought patterns, strongholds, and a period of refining. After completing this process, you will be relaunched as the new you, better and stronger, new and improved. "If any man be in Christ He is a new creature, old things are passed away behold all things are become new."(2 Corinthians 5:17 KJV) We can't be the new creature that He has called us to be until we allow old things to pass away and we embrace everything that comes with this new life. There is a process in between discovery and becoming but it takes commitment, focus, and faith. And guess what ladies….you can transform at any age!

If you desire to reconnect with who you were created to be before negative seeds tried to assassinate your destiny, this is for you. If you are experiencing frustration and discontent with where you are right now, this is for you. If you have been trying to evolve and move forward in destiny but still holding on to the past, this is for you! This book is a guide to assist you in your transformation as you are relaunched into your divine destiny packing an awareness of purpose, divine strategy, and a renewed and focused mind. This book is a 40 day journey of transparency, truth, healing, discovery and becoming everything you were created to be. It is all on the inside of you. Reach in and pull it out! I look forward to the new you.

Tips for Your 40 Day Journey

This book is comprised of five seven day cycles and five days of grace. Each week is designed to uproot seeds and strongholds that will hinder you from walking in your purpose as well as awaken you to the treasure that lies within. It is important that you are totally transparent and willing to surrender all so you may have the maximum experience possible. This is about a shift in your mind and a lifestyle change. Each day there will be a spiritual revelation, prayer, faith confession, and reflection questions. It is most effective by taking one day at a time, which includes daily prayer, faith confessions, journaling, and fasting from the strongholds in your life. At the end of each week, I encourage you to celebrate yourself and do something special no matter how small. I encourage you to join the 40 day challenge along with other women around the world. You will receive daily reminders and weekly encouraging emails. There will also be an opportunity to connect with other women who are a part of The New You Revolution. What you are about to embark on is not an easy task but a courageous one, and I promise you it will be rewarding. Let's go!

WEEK ONE

Breaking the Cycle of Condemnation

Condemnation places you in a cycle of bondage but the love of God gives you life!

I made a huge mistake! I should be further along. I am not walking in my purpose. I should have known better. These may be phrases that have entered your mind from time to time. While having these thoughts are a part of the normal process of rationalizing your current position in life, they should not linger and become a permanent residence in your mind. If they are not dealt with, these feelings will send you on a self-inflicted cycle of rehearsing lies from the enemy. The cycle is not of God and you don't have to receive it. The Bible says, "For God did not send his son into the world to condemn the world, but to save the world through him."(John 3:17) Because you love God and want to please Him the enemy will creep in when you make a mistake to plant the seed of condemnation. He wants you to believe that God doesn't love you and you are no longer a recipient of His saving grace. Remaining in the cycle of condemnation, will place you in bondage and keep you from the promises of God and living a life of freedom. God loves you and He wants you to experience the fulfilled and abundant life that He promised you. Many times we can't move forward in life because we are focusing on our past mistakes and unfruitful decisions instead of allowing God's grace, forgiveness, and unconditional love to cover us. Don't allow condemnation to become a stronghold in your life, but rather pull on God's strength to overcome.

If you want to become the new you and walk in your kingdom purpose, the cycle of condemnation has to be broken. This week, I want you to focus on all of the negative seeds that have been planted and all the strongholds that need to be uprooted and broken. I pray that you are honest with yourself and God and are willing to be purged. We will focus on the following topics: Acknowledgement; Detox - A Day of Release; I am Not Ashamed; Living Guilt Free; Forgiveness; Acceptance; and God's Love. This week is the foundation that will propel you forward in discovering and becoming the new you. Let's get started. The new you awaits!

DAY 1

Acknowledgement

Whatever you keep covered can never grow to its full potential. But whatever you acknowledge and expose can be nourished and given what it needs to come into full bloom.

Acknowledgment is the first step to breaking any addiction, habit, or negative cycle in your life. You must be honest with yourself and God regarding the areas in your life that need healing and deliverance. Your ability to be honest says that you are ready to let God deal with your heart. It is important to acknowledge those deep-seeded issues such as unforgiveness, bitterness, abandonment, rejection, lack of confidence, and pride so your healing process can begin. God loves you and He knows all about you so it is okay to come to Him naked and unashamed. He wants to make you new. In fact, He has been waiting for the opportunity where you allow Him access to your most vulnerable places. It is in your vulnerability that He will produce your greatest triumph. As women, it is easy for us to travel through life handling our day-to-day affairs all while living in bondage. We mask the hurt with more responsibility or what I call the "superwoman" mentality. We speak freedom and never walk in it. The enemy is crafty and he doesn't want you to be free and experience total victory. You must not live in denial another day but acknowledge every issue that has been gripping you all these years. You owe it to yourself to put on your big girl stilettos, look yourself in the mirror, and acknowledge. You have the power to be free, but you can't be set free from what you aren't willing to confront. So today, I want you to search your heart and do some self-inventory. Write down every issue from the past and present. Every issue that you know will hinder your destined place. Be aware of them all day. Speak them aloud and proclaim that you will be free. This may be uncomfortable, but be encouraged knowing that you are taking the first step in discovering and

becoming the new you!

Daily Scripture
"So be content with who you are, and don't put on airs.
God's strong hand is on you; he'll promote you at the right
time. Live care free before God; he is most careful with
you."
(1 Peter 5:7 MSG)

Prayer
Father, I come to you saying thank you. I thank you for the
opportunity to be real with myself and acknowledge that I
have issues that I need to be delivered and healed from. I
am open and available for you to do what needs to be done
so I can be healed, free, and walk in total victory. In Jesus
name, Amen.

Reflections
Write down every issue that you need God to heal so you
can be whole and ready to embrace your next dimension.

Every issue has a root. Write down what you believe is the
root of each issue.

What has acknowledging your issues done for you? How
did it make you feel?

Faith Confession
God, I acknowledge that I have issues that I need you to
fix. I open up and let my wall down so you can make me a
better woman. I recognize that denial has no place in my
life and is just a band-aid that is blocking my true healing

and deliverance. Because I have acknowledged this, I have started my process to becoming the new me.

DAY 2

Detox – A Day of Release

When you allow God to remove all the clutter and you release everything to Him, you increase your capacity for self-awareness thus producing change and growth.

During my time of transition, I was so confused and my spirit was not at peace. I would pray that God would settle me and allow me to come to a level of balance. While in conversation with God, I realized that there were many things that I had not released to Him. When God is taking you through the process of transformation, you will experience physical, spiritual, and emotional changes. Because you are literally being turned right side up, it is necessary that you find time to release. It is beneficial to you to allow a purging or releasing of every negative seed, energy, or habit that is residing in your soul. As women, we are emotional beings but we can no longer allow the negative things in our souls to dictate our emotions. Your flesh should not govern your spirit, but your spirit should govern your flesh. This is easier said than done, but it is a practice that you should adopt for it will change your life. You will no longer repeat the same cycle. You will no longer wrestle with strongholds that have been passed from generation to generation. God wants to do a refining work in you because it is time for you to be the woman that He created you to be. No more hindrances, no more excuses, and no more clutter!

Today you are to simply detox by releasing your hurt, anger, fears, and every unhealthy emotion to God. Reflect on every issue that you identified on yesterday, then look in the mirror and speak that you are no longer bound to it and you are free. Do not allow the enemy to trick you into believing that this will not work. You must believe that this is your appointed time for healing. Speak and pray! Pray and release! I want you to couple your confessions with prayer that God will meet you where you need Him most. I pray that your spiritual capacity is increased to receive and

believe that your healing and freedom has come. Visualize

every negative thing leaving you and that your spirit is free

to receive the new things that God desires to impart.

Daily Scripture
"He cuts off every branch in me that bears no fruit, while
every branch that does bear fruit he prunes so that it will
be even more fruitful."
(John 15:2 NIV)

Prayer
Father I thank you for purging me of the things that are
harmful to my spirit and my destiny. I thank you that I am
walking in total freedom and victory. Please grant me the
strength and the mind to stay focused. In Jesus name,
Amen.

Reflection
How do you believe detoxing will improve your life and
spiritual wellness?

Some people need a physical action to make this type of
change a reality. If this is you, write down your issues on
paper, recite your confessions, and throw each issue in the
trash individually and visualize that you are free from them.

*Remember to keep your mind in a posture of expectancy
and faith. Remove all doubt. Look into the mirror and
speak your confessions and journal how you feel at this
moment.

Faith Confession

Today I release every negative word that has been spoken over my life. I release every negative word that I declared into the atmosphere. Today is my day of detox through confession. I will no longer receive words that are harmful to my spirit. But I will continue to speak life.

DAY 3

I am Not Ashamed

Don't allow the enemy to silence you. Your silence frees no one, but your testimony coupled with the anointing will tear down walls and set the captives free.

I know the voice of shame firsthand. It speaks to you at night. It speaks to you while surrounded by a group of people who seem to have it altogether and tells you that you are an outcast. It advises you to never speak about your past. The voice of shame wants to silence you while it speaks loudly in your ear. The Bible says, "And they overcame him by the Blood of the Lamb and by the word of their testimony."(Revelation 12:11) You do know that you have a testimony, right? The enemy desires to play with your mind and cause you to feel ashamed so he can keep you from being free and from freeing others with your testimony. Every mistake produces a lesson and every lesson produces growth. Your mistakes can be lessons to someone else. Every sin that you have committed thrusts you in a posture with God where forgiveness and restoration can manifest. There is no reason for you to feel ashamed about anything that you have done. God loves you, He created you, and He knows all about you. The wonderful thing about our father is that He wants you to come to Him and release it all to Him because He has a plan for your life. Your sin doesn't disqualify you from receiving His love, grace, mercy, and forgiveness. He will transform your life so that where you were incomplete, you are now whole. If you were ever ashamed you will now be free to embrace what you have gone through. You must stand in confidence knowing that whatever happened in your past has worked for your good. Do not allow the enemy to rob you of your testimony and fulfilling your kingdom purpose. The spirit of shame is not of God. It is just another way the enemy is trying to keep you from arriving at your destiny.

Today, I challenge you to stand boldly and proclaim that you are not ashamed of your journey. In fact, you celebrate where you came from and where you are right now. You survived the process! Tell yourself that you are an overcomer. Today is your day to be free from shame and walk in God's grace. Believe that God's grace is sufficient for you. Victory is yours.

Daily Scripture

"So now there is no condemnation for those who belong to Christ Jesus. And because you belong to him, the power of the life-giving spirit has freed you from the power of sin that leads to death."
(Romans 8:1-2 NLT)

Prayer

Father, I pray that you release me from the feelings of shame that once had me bound. If I am the cause for remaining in a cycle of shame, show me how to accept that I no longer have to bear those feelings. I pray that you reveal to me the testimony that lies in everything I have been through. I thank you for your grace and mercy and for turning my bad into good. I am on my way to recovery and I thank you! In Jesus name, Amen.

Reflection

Why do you feel ashamed?

Write down all the things you feel ashamed about. Then write down how each thing can be used as a testimony to bless someone else.

If you are really bold, pray for an opportunity to share with someone at least one thing you feel or felt ashamed about and how God turned your shame into a testimony!

Faith Confession
I am not ashamed of my past or what I have been through. The enemy can no longer hold me in bondage. I am free today to tell my testimony so that it will free someone else. Everything I have been through has made me who I am today.

DAY 4

Living Guilt Free

There is no need to wrestle with something that Jesus took on the cross.

So you made a mistake, a bad decision, or hurt someone you cared about. Now guilt has set in and you feel unworthy of God's best. Ladies, guilt is a natural emotion that we have all experienced or will experience as a result of some form of wrong doing. It is a part of the process to emotional healing but guilt was never meant to cause you to live a defeated life. It is one of the major weapons that the enemy uses against you to keep you from walking in freedom, and living an abundant and purposed life. Yes, it is important to become aware, admit, and accept what you did wrong. But it is not for you to wallow in it but to ask for forgiveness, learn, make the necessary adjustments, and move forward. If you hurt someone apologize and move on. This will free you and at the same time allow you to feel a sense of accomplishment for doing the right thing. However, it is not up to you to make that person forgive you, all you can do is apologize and keep them in prayer. You cannot allow someone else to hold you hostage to guilt because of blame or manipulation. Do not allow the enemy or others to cause feelings of guilt to replay in your mind. Instead of rehearsing the negative things that are sent to destroy you, renew your mind daily with the word of God and speak healthy and positive affirmations. You will no longer feel guilty for the mistakes that you made. You will no longer feel guilty for being who God created you to be. You will live guilt free! So today, I want you to meditate on how good it feels that the weight of guilt has been released from your life. I want you to declare that guilt will no longer keep you in bondage. Meditate on God's word knowing that He loves you no matter what!

Daily Scripture
"Even if we feel guilty, God is greater than our feelings,
and he knows everything."
(1 John 3:20 NLT)

Prayer
Father, I thank you for freeing me from guilt and covering
me with the grace to move forward. I thank you that the
shackles that were once holding me captive have been
broken. I believe that you called me to live a life free of
guilt and full of love. Because of you, today I live guilt
free! In Jesus name, Amen.

Reflection
Why have you allowed guilt to enter your life?

Write down everything that you are guilty about. Then
write down why you are guilty. If your feelings of guilt are
due to manipulation from another person, disconnect
yourself immediately so you can be healed and free. If you
are the source of feeling guilty, give yourself permission to
let it go.

Journal your thoughts and feelings at this moment.

Faith Confession
I recognize and understand that I am human and I am not
perfect. Yes, I made mistakes but I am no longer bound to
them. I am moving forward toward my destined place. God
loves me and He wants the best for me. I am worthy of
God's best and my abundant life is now! I am living my life
guilt free!

DAY 5

There is Freedom in Forgiveness

Forgiveness is one of the best gifts you can give yourself. For forgiveness allows you to release, exhale, and live.

Have you heard the common phrase, "I will forgive but I will never forget?" I have. God revealed to me that it is a dangerous line between forgiving and forgetting. Be careful that in not forgetting you don't unknowingly continue to harbor unforgiveness. Believe me, it happens. Holding on to unforgiveness enslaves you and hinders your access to freedom. God is the ultimate forgiver. He sent His son Jesus to die on the cross for our sins so that we could have a right to salvation which is wrapped in forgiveness. Forgiveness is a gift from God. God doesn't have to forgive us, but He does it over and over again. It is just who He is. "For I will forgive their wickedness and will remember their sins no more."(Hebrews 8:12) If God can forgive and forget our sins, then we must forgive and forget what others have done to us. What does it mean to forgive? It means to leave behind or fail to give attention to a particular matter. It is time that you forgive and leave behind what others have done to you. "For if you forgive other people when they sin against you, your heavenly Father will also forgive you."(Matthew 6:14) Don't harbor unforgiveness in your heart. It stunts your growth and eats away at your spiritual and natural wellness. Unforgiveness leads to bitterness, anger, and resentment. Don't you want to be free? I know, you may be saying, "You don't know what they did to me." But forgiveness is not about the other person, it is about your freedom, growth, healing, and ability to move forward.

As women, we struggle with forgiving ourselves. It is as if we have programmed our minds to believe that not forgiving ourselves for something continues to hold us responsible and accountable for it. It is okay to admit and acknowledge, but it is not okay to be a disservice to

yourself by not accepting what God has given

you…FORGIVENESS. If God has forgiven you, you can

forgive yourself. Today is all about opening your heart and

availing yourself to forgiveness. Ask the Lord for

forgiveness, forgive others, and forgive yourself. You will

feel so much better, I promise you! Be free today!

Daily Scripture
"If we confess our sins, he is faithful and just and will forgive us our sins and purify us from all unrighteousness."
(1 John 1:9 NIV)

Prayer
Father, I thank you for sending your son Jesus to die on the cross that my sins would be forgiven. I thank you for forgiving me and every sin and disobedient way. I am grateful to you for teaching me how to forgive and showing me how to forgive myself. Thanks God!

Reflection
Do you harbor unforgiveness? Why?

If you have not taken the time to ask God for forgiveness, take the time and do it today.

If there is anyone you have not forgiven, take the time today and make it right. Make a phone call or write a letter and let them know that you forgive them. If you are unable to contact them, speak it aloud.

Today, I challenge you to write yourself a letter of forgiveness. How do you feel?

Faith Confession

Today, I open up my heart and receive God's forgiveness. I release unforgiveness from my life and I forgive everyone who has hurt me. And today, I give myself a precious gift and I forgive myself!

DAY 6

Acceptance

In life you are constantly evolving. In order to move into your next phase of life, you must accept what is in order to embrace what is to come.

Why does it seem like acceptance is one of the hardest things to do? To accept simply means that you agree or you come to terms with what is. Acceptance doesn't mean that a particular situation is right. Acceptance doesn't have to be what you desire or want but acceptance is necessary for the process of healing, growth, and development. The lack of acceptance can be fueled by fear, hurt, rejection and denial. Oftentimes we have this picture in our minds of how our lives should have been or what we should have accomplished by a certain time. When what we have built in our minds as reality is not fulfilled, acceptance of what is has to take place. Until you relinquish your desires and the reality you have created in your mind, you will never be able to live and let the divine guide you as He is in control. It is important that you mature to the place where you understand that you are not perfect and that you will make mistakes. Freedom comes when you accept your past, accept your now, and understand your future. It doesn't mean that you become comfortable but when you accept, you invite the flow of God into your life. The enemy can no longer keep you in a cycle of denial, guilt, unforgiveness, or shame. Acceptance cancels the manipulation of the enemy and you will no longer be in a tug of war with God but in agreement with His will for your life.

Today, I want you to open up your spirit and accept what is. Accept the things you cannot change, accept what you need to change, and accept God's will for your life. There may be many things you wanted in life but it just wasn't a part of God's plan. When you accept it you allow the peace of God to be your portion! You must meditate on acceptance and free yourself.

Daily Scripture
"Rejoice in the Lord always. I will say it again: Rejoice! Let your gentleness be evident to all. The Lord is near. Do not be anxious about anything, but in every situation, by prayer and petition, with thanksgiving, present your requests to God. And the peace of God, which transcends all understanding, will guard your hearts and your minds in Christ Jesus."
(Philippians 4:6-7 NIV)

Prayer
Father, you know all things and I believe that you have a plan for my life. I know that all things are working together for my good. So I accept where I am right now, and I accept your will for my life. Thank you for showing me the power in acceptance. In Jesus name, Amen.

Reflection
Do you have difficulty accepting? Why?

Think of everything in your life right now that you need to accept in order to have peace and move forward in your purpose. Write them down on index cards or post them on your wall or refrigerator. Recite them every day and accept them.

Faith Confession
Today, I choose to accept what I cannot change. I accept what I've done. I accept where I am now. I accept where I am going and because I have accepted, I am free from condemnation. I invite God's flow into my life.

DAY 7

God's Love

When you experience God's love it is like exhaling for the first time…indescribable and life-changing!

Do you know what it feels like for God to love on you?
Have you ever experienced loneliness due to the absence of
people but weren't alone because you felt the loving arms
of your heavenly father? Do you struggle with intimacy
with God because you truly have not allowed His love to
penetrate your heart? Or do you confuse His love with what
you have received from others? God's love transcends
time, it moves beyond flaws, it penetrates the depths of
your soul. God's love is unlike any other. Do not reject His
love based on your love experiences with others. God
desires for you to move from knowing of Him to truly
knowing Him, which comes through a love relationship.

Everything I thought I knew about love changed and is still changing when I discovered the love of God.

Love is a word that is spoken loosely and often misused. In today's society, everyone says they love you and most of the time it is not true love. However, everything God does is because of love. In fact, God is love. His love is sincere; His love is powerful; His love is perfect; His love is everlasting; His love is unconditional; and His love endures all things. When we make mistakes, the enemy and man sends condemnation, but God covers us in His love. Yes, He may chastise us but God chastises those whom He loves. The Bible says that love covers a multitude of sin. You see, love is powerful. I want to encourage you that God loves you no matter what. God's love is not situational. He doesn't fall in and out of love with you. His love remains! It is to your benefit to receive and grab hold to His love and use it as your strength to move forward.

As you embrace the new you, understand that some people just don't have the capacity to love you on the level that you need. This is okay. Simply love them as God has commanded you. You don't have to like everything a person does but you are commanded to love them with the love of Christ. When you extend the love of Christ to others you will feel joy and peace and you operate in purpose. God's love stretches beyond faults, attitudes, egos, pride, and disagreements. God's love extends compassion and loves in spite of. When you really experience God's love the enemy will no longer be able to keep you in a cycle of condemnation and you will no longer be bound to the opinions of others.

Today, I want you to meditate on God's love and remember how it has brought purpose, freedom, and change to your life. I also want you to pray for ways to extend the love of Christ to others. The love of Christ will be a turning point in your life as well as the lives of others.

Step outside of yourself for a moment and allow God to love on you as you love yourself; then love the people of God.

Daily Scripture
"For God so loved the world, that he gave his only begotten Son, that whosoever believeth in him should not perish, but have everlasting life."
(John 3:16 KJV)

Prayer
Father, I thank you for loving me with an unconditional love. I thank you for being the lover of my soul and showing me what real love is. I pray that you would teach me how to operate in your love. Thank you for counting me worthy. In Jesus name, Amen.

Reflection
Do you feel loved by God? Why or Why not?

Ask yourself, have you truly allowed yourself to experience and receive God's love? Write down some of the ways you have experienced His love.

What are ways you can extend the love of Christ to others?

Meditate on scriptures about God's love

Faith Confession
I am loved because I am loved by God. God's love is able to break every cycle in my life. Because of God's love I have been freed from the bondage of condemnation. I am free to receive God's love and extend His love to others.

CELEBRATE YOURSELF!

Congratulations! You have completed the first week of your 40 day journey. So, it is time for you to celebrate yourself. It is okay to take some much needed ME time. Do something special for yourself today. Go see a movie, enjoy a massage, and soak in a candlelit bath while enjoying some tea. Do whatever you can to celebrate you! You are on your way to becoming the New You! It's a revolution!

WEEK TWO

Identity Crisis: Rediscovering the Hidden Treasure

———————————————————✖———————————————————

Life is a journey of discovering what has been hidden in your spirit. You just need to reconnect to what you already know and who you already are.

What adjectives come to mind when you think of a treasure chest? I think of valuable, priceless, huge, and private. If you are in search of a treasure, once you discover it you will guard and treat it as a valuable gem. So why do we allow the enemy and people to tamper with our treasure? Is it because we haven't discovered it or because we haven't come into the knowledge of its value?

"The enemy comes to steal, kill, and destroy, but I have come that you would have life and have it more abundantly."(John 10:10) It is the enemies desire to steal your identity, kill your dreams, and destroy your destiny. He is very crafty as he will attempt to manipulate your mind into believing that you don't know who you are and that you are void of purpose. He tries to keep you in a cycle of not knowing who you are through the strongholds of fear, confusion, rejection, doubt, and lack of clarity. "For I know the plans I have for you saith the Lord, plans to prosper you and not to harm you, plans to give you hope and a future."(Jeremiah 29:11) The Lord has great plans for your life and He has already hidden the blueprint on the inside of you. You are not without purpose and your identity is not stolen. It is just hidden under all of the labels that have been attached to you. It is imperative that you reacquaint yourself with the real you so you won't fall prey to the trap of trying to duplicate someone else's identity. Your identity lies in Christ. The more you get to know Christ, the more you know who you are. On your journey to rediscovery, you will reach a pivotal point where you will experience frustration and lack of fulfillment. This will bring you to a place of questions. Those questions will bring you to a revelation and the revelation will bring you to a state of consciousness; a new understanding of who you are. Do not dismiss your dreams for they reflect who you are.

Now that you have dealt with the cycle of condemnation, it is time to reconnect to your true identity in Christ. God created you and He knows your beginning and your end. He desires for you to stand in the unique identity that only you can bring to life.

This week I want you to embark on a journey of recapturing your identity through rediscovering your hidden treasure. We will explore the topics: I am God's Masterpiece; Uniquely You; No More Labels; The Power of Rejection; Validation; Removing the Mask; and Love Yourself. What you are in search of is not where you have been looking. Redirect your search and take a journey into the deep places of your spirit. Are you ready?

DAY 8

I am God's Masterpiece

An artist's masterpiece may receive several interpretations from onlookers, but the expression of the artist and the purpose of the piece never changes.

A masterpiece is said to be a person's greatest work and is done with excellence and mastery skill. God does all things well! He created you in His image and likeness. When He created you and me, He created a masterpiece. You are the manifestation of His spoken expression. He has numbered every hair on your head. Look at the time and attention God took in creating you. You are the apple of His eye. Can't you just visualize God looking at you and smiling at what He created? When you read the word of God and you truly internalize it, your self-worth will sky rocket. Have you ever thought that the reason why you don't walk with confidence and authority is because you don't know the truth about who you are? You are God's

44

most prized possession and the enemy doesn't want you to discover or be reminded of your identity in Christ. When you know who you are and that you belong to Christ, there is an authority that comes on you that tells the enemy to BACK DOWN. Doesn't it make you excited to know that you are extremely valuable to God? "You are a royal priesthood and a chosen generation and He has called you out of darkness into his marvelous light."(1 Peter 2:9) That means He cares about you and He has a plan for your life. You must know that you are a child of God and that He has called you friend.

Today, I want you to walk with joy and authority knowing that you are God's masterpiece. I want you to read the word and make it personal to you. Don't just read the word like pages in a book but read it to learn who God is and discover who you are. Christ paid the price for you so no price tag could ever determine your worth. You are a masterpiece and that my dear is priceless!

Daily Scripture
"For we are God's workmanship, created in Christ Jesus to do good works, which God prepared in advance for us to do."
(Ephesians 2:10 NIV)

Prayer
Father, I thank you for creating me in your image and giving me an identity in you. I pray that you will lead and guide me on my journey of rediscovering who I am. I thank you for loving me and calling me friend.

Reflection
Do you believe you are God's masterpiece? What hinders you from fully operating as God's masterpiece?

Write down as many scriptures as you can that relate to God's creation and what He says about you. Read them and recite them aloud.

Faith Confession
I am God's workmanship, His masterpiece, and His skillful handiwork. God created me exactly how He wants me to be. I am valuable to God and my identity lies in Christ. I will walk with my head held high in the authority given by God. I am God's child and I am blessed.

DAY 9

Uniquely Me

Being unique says you embrace your truth. It requires you to be courageous enough to take a stand and BE!

Identity is the collective aspect of the set of characteristics by which a thing is definitively recognizable or known. You carry spiritual DNA that is unique to you. God made you an original. Your personality and characteristics are distinctive. What you consider flaws are all a part of who God made you to be. When you ask most people who they are, oftentimes they answer with what they do, what title or position they have, or what their purpose is. Your identity is not what you do but who you are in Christ. When you allow your calling and assignment to be your identity, it leads to false validation and approval. Others determine their identity based on who they are connected with and who they admire and desire to become.

God didn't create you to be a carbon copy of anyone else. He created you to be one of a kind. There is a specific sparkle that you have and there is greatness inside you that others need that only you can give. It is important that you dig through all the layers and discover your treasure so your authentic self can shine through.

As you evolve and grow older in wisdom, your uniqueness will be about the total you. Even your quirky ways become what makes you unique. For example, think about that one thing that you love but others find it completely boring or that quality that others call a flaw, but it is actually your uniqueness shining through. It is time that you embrace all of you and live authentically. Don't try to be what others think you should be. For being less than your authentic self will keep you in bondage and unfulfilled. So what if you have a dry sense of humor. So what if you snort when you laugh. It is all a part of your wonderful personality! Don't be afraid to be you. That is what God desires for you to do. Remember, on your journey to the new you, it may be challenging to embrace your uniqueness in its fullness because you are changing, shifting, refocusing, and elevating but when you arrive at destination "new you", it will all come together.

So today I want you to embrace your uniqueness and be proud of who you are. Be determined to be the best YOU that you can be! Don't try to walk in stilettos when you know you are a flat. Wear the flats and keep it moving.

Daily Scripture
"For you created my inmost being; you knit me together in my mother's womb. I praise you because I am fearfully and wonderfully made; your works are wonderful, I know that full well."
(Psalm 139:13-14 NIV)

Prayer
Father, I thank you for creating me in a special and unique way. Thank you for giving me my unique personality and giving me the ability to embrace it. Thank you for giving me unique gifts and abilities that I can share with the world to bring you glory. In Jesus name, Amen.

Reflection
Do you struggle with letting your uniqueness shine?

Today, I want you to write who you are. Write down your characteristics and personality traits that make you unique.

If you had to be a purse, which one would you be…a hobo, a clutch, or a tote? Call a friend and share and encourage them do the same.

Faith Confession

I am uniquely me. I am who God says I am. I am fearfully and wonderfully made. I embrace my uniqueness and I understand that what I consider flaws are still a part of God's wonderful creation. I am a designer's original and I rock!

DAY 10

No More Labels

Labels are deceiving and may not represent the quality of what is inside. Move beyond labels and discover truth.

Society in general is heavily driven by perceptions, labels and judgments. Oftentimes people have preconceived thoughts and opinions before they even get to know who you are. We label people based on their past, mistakes, appearance, status, and even their church. Labels are like leaches that grab a hold to you and drain your identity. In order to rediscover the treasure within and embody your true identity, you must remove the labels. I am reminded of the woman in the Bible with the issue of blood. She was labeled for her condition and it kept her in fear and bondage and perhaps feelings of rejection kept her from her healing for twelve years. But I believe that one day her desire to discover who she really was outweighed the pain of her labels and it led her to Jesus where she was healed. Have you ever been labeled? Has that label gripped you so deeply that you believed it? Is it possible that God allows you to endure the placement of labels just to bring you to a place of discovery, certainty, faith and promotion? I say absolutely! My sister every woman in the Bible who had a label had a testimony. The Samaritan woman; the woman with the issue of blood; the woman with the alabaster box; the adulterous woman...they all were labeled but had a testimony of freedom. God will divinely interrupt your life by allowing a label to attempt to brand you, but not break you. It might cause you pain, but it will reignite passion. Whatever you are passionate about you will pursue. When you pursue you discover, when you discover there is room for certainty, and once you are certain confidence comes. Once you are confident, there is freedom and promotion.

If you are reading this book, it is time for to push forward and remove the labels and be free. You are not your past, you are not your mistakes, you are not your environment, and you are not what others have labeled you as. It is time to uproot the negative words and labels that have been placed on you. Do not let the chatter take your focus. You may not be who they think, but you are all that God said. What you possess on the inside is far more valuable than any label or price tag. Today, I want you to remove the labels and be free.

Daily Scripture
"The Spirit himself testifies with our spirit that we are God's children. Now if we are children, then we are heirs— heirs of God and co-heirs with Christ, if indeed we share in his sufferings in order that we may also share in his glory. I consider that our present sufferings are not worth comparing with the glory that will be revealed in us."
(Romans 8:16-18 NIV)

Prayer
Father, I thank you for you don't judge me and you love me in spite of. I am grateful that regardless of the labels that man has tried to place on me that I only carry one label and that is a child of God. Thank you Jesus. Amen.

Reflection

Today, I want you to release yourself from every label and negative word. Write down every label and negative word and then beside it write I AM NOT

_____.

How have labels affected you? How can you overcome the hurt of labels?

Faith Confession

I am no longer bound to the labels that man has placed on me. I am not defined by what others think of me. I am who God said I am. I do not have to live up to the labels and expectations of my peers rather only fulfill the word of God over my life. No more labels.

DAY 11

The Power of Rejection

It is through the experience of rejection that you discover your greatest asset.

No! We don't need you on our team. I'm sorry, you didn't get the job. We chose a more qualified candidate. It was good while it lasted but I've found someone else. Can you relate to these words? To those who have never wrestled with the spirit of rejection, they are just expressions of honest feelings. However, to those who are fighting to overcome rejection, it is the fruit of a deeper seed. Rejection starts as a seed and can give birth to several other strongholds such as low self-esteem, depression, and lack of confidence. Many of you may have experienced rejection from your family, friends, spouse, your job, and even your church. If it is not dealt with, the seed of rejection will continue to grow and attempt to snatch your identity. Rejection can be hurtful, but you can be free and find the power that lies within it. I remember being in a situation and the Lord gave me an assignment, but I was rejected. I cried to God asking for an answer. Why did rejection frequently show up in my life? And the Lord said, "If you want to know how to become confident, it is through rejection." Say, what? Those words the Lord spoke to me changed my entire perspective. I get it. When you have endured so much rejection the last thing you want to experience is more rejection. Nevertheless, being rejected will bring confidence once you understand that rejection is really redirection. The more you are rejected and isolated the more you are redirected and pushed to get in the face of God and find out what He says about you. Rejection strengthens your relationship with God, increases your confidence, and further assists you in recognizing your greatness.

It is time that you flip the script and find the power in rejection. It can no longer be a stronghold in your life. There is nothing wrong with you. Rejection is your proof of your greatness. Everyone cannot handle who you are and it is okay. Don't adjust who you are or what you do because others can't handle you. It has to happen in order for your **greater** to happen. Even Jesus was rejected and He was the savior of the world. But He recognized who He was and what God sent him to do. He didn't allow rejection to have power over him because He had power over it. Today, I want you to release yourself from the wounds of rejection. Forgive those who rejected you and be free. Thank God today for showing you how to reclaim your power!

Daily Scripture
"Jesus is 'the stone you builders rejected, which has become the cornerstone.'"
(Acts 4:11 NLT)

Prayer
Father, I thank you for showing me the deception in rejection. Thank you for revealing the power that I have through the spirit of rejection. I ask that you will continue to allow me to govern my emotions and to gain true deliverance that the spirit of rejection will not find an open door. In Jesus name, Amen.

Reflection
Have you experienced rejection?

How has rejection affected your search for identity?

How can you turn your experience of rejection into power?

Faith Confession:
Today, I understand that rejection is divine confirmation of my greatness. No longer will I feel sad because someone rejected me. I will not allow my emotions to take over, but instead I will find the power in the situation. Although man rejects me, I know that God has accepted me and called me great!

DAY 12

Validation

When you make a decision to trust the God in you the need for validation will no longer exist.

I remember being in college when the new semester approached. In order to attend class, each student was required to be validated. Validation meant that you met all financial requirements needed to attend the university that year. It almost separated the students into two categories: those who were validated and able to attend classes; and those who were not. It was a red flag that there was an issue present. As women, we often struggle with the need for validation. I know I did. We desire to feel a sense of belonging, to feel approved or accepted. There is a void that is present and man's approval will not fill it. If you are in search of validation, ask yourself why. Why do you value someone else's identity and opinion over your own?

A life-changing situation and a season of transition can produce the pursuit for validation. It is like you want to make sure that you are not crazy. You want to feel normal again. But you must be careful because seeking validation from the wrong source can lead to false praise, co-dependency, and a continued lack of self-confidence. God has already validated you and you don't need affirmation from anyone else. In order to end the search for validation, you must be confident in yourself. Webster's dictionary states that to validate is to recognize, establish or illustrate the worthiness or legitimacy of a thing. Wow! So when you are in need of validation you are saying to yourself that you need someone else to establish or recognize your worth. Not so! The Bible says, "And the God of all grace, who called you to his eternal glory in Christ, after you have suffered a little while, will himself restore you and make you strong, firm and steadfast."(1 Peter 5:10 NIV) You must discover your identity; stand on it, and trust who God has made you to be. You must hold yourself in high esteem

and know that you are worth more than man's approval.

Your identity is priceless.

Today, I want you to reflect on your self-worth and

what you offer to the world. Believe that God has already

validated you and that is all you need.

Daily Scripture
"Being confident of this very thing, that he which hath begun a good work in you will perform it until the day of Jesus Christ'"
(Philippians 1:6 KJV)

Prayer
Father, I thank you for making a covenant with me and establishing me. Thank you for revealing to me that validation and approval from others are not important. In Jesus name, Amen.

Reflection
Do you seek validation or approval from man? Why?

Do you believe you are worthy of God's Best?

What can you do to honor yourself and your value?

Faith Confession

I am worthy of God's best. I will no longer seek validation from man because God has already established me and given me His stamp of approval. I don't need the opinions of others to make me feel good about myself. I honor and value who God has created me to be.

DAY 13

Removing the Mask

To remove your mask says you have matured to a place of transparency which will give birth to a new level of understanding and thanksgiving.

Have you ever attended a masquerade ball? Everyone comes dressed with their black and white tuxedos and beautiful ball gowns and everyone wears a mask the entire time. No one can distinguish one person from another. The guests attend the party with the intentions of deceiving those in attendance by not exposing who they really are, but it is all in fun. My question to you is, "what mask are you wearing today?" Is it the same mask you wore yesterday? When will the **real _woman_** behind the mask be revealed?

Wearing a mask is never fun but, the truth of the matter is that, we all have worn a mask at some point in our lives. Some call it "faking it till you make it" and some call it not wearing your feelings on your sleeve. But whatever the case, your journey of life should not be motivated by hidden identity. Many times we don't know how to cope and deal with situations so we retreat and begin to cover up our true feelings with a mask. We hide behind a facade pretending that everything is okay when it really is not. We allow things to become our identity so we won't have to deal with our issues and really discover who we are. Some of you wear the mask of "I don't need a man", or "I'm doing me", or I am free and healed" and all of that is good if it is truth. So if in fact you are not being truthful, masks are all wrong when at the core of you is hurt, low self-esteem, and bitterness. When we mask our issues, we will start craving things that will only delay our process of healing and wholeness. Although it is common for many to attach themselves to material possessions as a form of identity, clinging to tangible possessions can keep you from a supernatural deliverance. Yes, deliverance! God is the answer to all the hurt and disappointment we have experienced. He wants to get to the core of you so that healing and deliverance can begin. Some of you just need to breathe again. Open up to Him, be vulnerable and let Him love you and show you how to breathe again. When you accepted Christ as your personal Lord and Savior you automatically became His child. You instantaneously become a new creature and old things are passed away. You don't have to be bound to those heart issues any longer. You don't have to be bound by situations or the masks that you have become so comfortably attached to for God has freed you. You must choose to remove the mask and be free.

As a woman of God, if you ever want to operate in true purpose, you must be honest and admit that you are wearing a mask; identify the mask; deal with the mask and from where it originated; and destroy it. Once you have destroyed it, you may now expose who you really are. You will never discover your true identity until you remove the mask. It can be a painful process but it is necessary. It is time for you to be free for real. Today, I encourage you to remove the mask and start your journey to wholeness. I want you to intentionally become aware of what you are using as a mask and begin the process to removing.

Daily Scripture

"For the Lord is the Spirit, and wherever the Spirit of the Lord is, there is freedom. So all of us who have had that veil removed can see and reflect the glory of the Lord. And the Lord-who is the Spirit-makes us more and more like him as we are changed into his glorious image."
(2 Corinthians 3:17-18 NLT)

Prayer

Father I thank you for bringing me to a place of awareness. Thank you for being patient with me as I remove the masks. I am grateful for your love and for setting me free. In Jesus name, Amen.

Reflection

Are you wearing a mask today? Why?

Write down every mask that you wear. Look yourself in the mirror and say,
Today, I remove the mask of _____.

Faith Confession

Today, I acknowledge that I wear a mask and it is keeping me from walking in my true identity. But today I remove the masks by the power of the Holy Spirit and I am healed, whole, and free!

DAY 14

Love Yourself

You can't love God and not love His creation. To love yourself is to love God.

So day fourteen is here and it is all about loving yourself. Rediscovering your hidden treasure means that you have opened up your spirit and reconnected to the spirit of God. Do you truly love yourself or are you on a journey to increase in self-love? When you love yourself it means that you accept yourself as you are. It means you have come to terms with the aspects of yourself that you cannot change. Wow! I had to really look at my own love meter and it was way off. Sometimes we say we love ourselves, but we still accept the same toxic behaviors from others; yet we love ourselves enough to wear the finest clothing. It occurred to me that some of us may be loving parts of ourselves but we haven't completely given ourselves to what God desires…unconditional love. I realized that I was comparing who I am to what my life has become by way of circumstance as a measure to loving myself. I couldn't love myself holistically because I blamed myself for the mistakes I made. I became the problem to save the image of others in my life that I desperately wanted to receive love from and, in turn, I didn't honor and love me! Ladies, love must begin from within and it will exude honor and reverence. Love can free you from the enemy within. Loving yourself is powerful and is the key to the new you!

When you truly discover your identity and your hidden treasure, you will have an increased love for yourself. It is a wonderful feeling to wake up every morning and look in the mirror and like what you see; not from a material or superficial perspective but holistically. You are the manifestation of His word so to love yourself is to love and respect the creative mind of God. If you love yourself you will no longer allow people and issues to penetrate and contaminate your spirit. Your standards and expectations will rise to a new level. You will no longer except less than God's best. Your esteem, confidence, love for others, all stem from your love for yourself. Love says you accept who you are and you allow it to lead you into true fulfillment. Your hair, beauty, outfit or job does not define you but YOU define it. You have a treasure inside you that is worth more than money; not possessions, not people, not status, but LOVE. Invest in yourself beyond high-end department stores and superficial images. Invest in self-love as it is sure to yield a great return. Today, I want you to exhale and love yourself. Give yourself permission to love you!

Daily Scripture:
"And so we know and rely on the love God has for us. God is love. Whoever lives in love lives in God, and God in them. This is how love is made complete among us so that we will have confidence on the day of judgment: In this world we are like Jesus. There is no fear in love. But perfect love drives out fear, because fear has to do with punishment. The one who fears is not made perfect in love. We love because he first loved us. Whoever claims to love

God yet hates a brother or sister is a liar. For whoever does not love their brother and sister, whom they have seen, cannot love God, whom they have not seen. And he has given us this command: Anyone who loves God must also love their brother and sister."
(1 John 4: 16-21 NIV)

Prayer
Father, I thank you for loving me unconditionally and teaching me how to love myself. I will no longer receive things that bring dishonor to me. Today, I love myself with a greater love. In Jesus name, Amen.

Reflection
Do you truly love yourself?

What can you do to honor and respect yourself more?

Write yourself a love letter.

Faith Confession
Today, I exhale and I love myself. I will walk with confidence, and I will not allow anyone to disrespect my hidden treasure.

CELEBRATE YOURSELF!

Congratulations! You have completed the second week of your 40 day journey. So, it is time to celebrate the discovery of your hidden treasure. It is okay to take some much needed ME time. Do something special for yourself. Go see a movie, enjoy a massage, and soak in a candlelit bath while enjoying some tea. Do whatever you can to celebrate you! You are one step closer to becoming the New You! It's a revolution!

WEEK THREE

The Quest for Purpose

Purpose is not a replacement for identity but it is the next layer of the foundation for true awareness and understanding of the plan of God for your life.

Have you ever been asked to assist someone with a specific task or instruction and midway through you stopped and asked, "Why am I doing this again?" It is amazing how we can be actively working on a task, assignment, or project and we don't even fully understand the purpose for which we are working. Purpose is an entity that individuals are desperately pursuing. Many desire to know what they were created to do on the earth. Have you ever asked yourself these questions: Where do I fit?; Where do I belong?; Who am I?; What did God create me to do? These are questions that I had often asked myself. It is okay to ask yourself these questions but, more importantly, God is who you need to ask. God created you in His image and likeness and He placed His purpose for your life on the inside of you before you were born. God is a God of strategy and order. He didn't just create you to exist but He created you with a purpose, however; purpose is not your identity although the two are connected. In addition, your assignment is not your purpose although it is the vehicle that God uses to assist you in fulfilling purpose. Your purpose is simply the reason for which you exist. Do you know your purpose? Many of us are gliding through life without the activation of purpose. I say this because it is not that purpose doesn't exist but it is that you haven't realized it and come into the understanding of what you are purposed to do. Some of you are probably unaware that you are walking in it. Are you looking for your purpose to be supercalifragilisticexpialidocious?! Oftentimes we compare what others are doing to what we are doing and what has been framed as important to determine if our purpose is relevant; BIG MISTAKE! Your purpose is relevant because it was intricately created by God! Perhaps your purpose is to be an encourager and a catalyst for strength and renewal; perhaps your purpose is to be a mediator and bring unity; or maybe your purpose is to offer healing through therapeutic services. Whatever it is, the world needs what you have! Don't believe the hype that purpose is this grandiose thing like being a worldwide televangelist or being a renowned millionaire or a media mogul like Oprah. The truth is that once you tap into purpose and you flow in it your world is transformed. Oprah did not just become a media mogul. I'm sure she discovered her purpose by way of process and worked it. As you move and as you seek, you will collide with purpose. So, this week, I want to encourage you in your quest for purpose. You must remember that purpose evolves as you are transformed. On our journey to purpose, we will explore the following topics such as What's Your Motivation; Conversations with God; Consistency; Obedience; Relationships; The

Awakening; and Forward March. I am excited about this

week, are you? Let's go!

DAY 15

What's Your Motivation?

When you are one with God, your motivation comes from that which is within that empowers you and strengthens you to move in the purpose of His plan.

The absence of purpose will cause you to feel an unexplainable void in your spirit. You begin to reach at ideas, people, and systems in an effort to fill the void. But purpose has to be discovered internally. It is a wonderful decision to seek after purpose but the question remains, what is your motivation? What is propelling your seek? Are you in a season of discovery, transition or restoration? Are you being led by God? It is important to evaluate your motives and intentions for seeking purpose. You might be saying to yourself that this sounds a bit ridiculous. Isn't seeking my purpose a good thing? Yes, seeking your purpose is something you must do, but purpose has also been distorted and abused. It is being used as some sort of measuring stick of greatness, status, or superiority. But that is not the will of God. Your purpose should drive you to fulfill the will of God for your life and bring glory to His name. Yes, discovering your purpose may connect you to the thing that will bring you wealth and prosperity but what it brings shouldn't motivate you, for purpose itself should be your motivation. Are you seeking purpose with the mindset that it will solve all your problems? As you are on your quest for purpose be sure to evaluate your motives. Continue to stay connected to God in prayer that His will remains your focus. Let Jesus be your example as His motivation was to accomplish the will of His father.

Today, I want you to free yourself from tying your purpose to achievement and status. Be honest with yourself about your motives and intentions. The truth is that purpose is not a replacement for dealing with your issues. Let your motivation be your desire to be complete in God.

Daily Scripture

"Meanwhile, the disciples were urging Jesus, "Rabi, eat something." But Jesus replied, "I have a kind of food you know nothing about." "Did someone bring him food while we were gone?" the disciples asked each other. Then Jesus explained: "My nourishment comes from doing the will of God, who sent me, and from finishing his work."
(John 4:31-34NLT)

Prayer

Father, I give you thanks for leading me on a quest for purpose. I thank you for challenging me to evaluate my motives and intentions. I thank you for creating me with a special and unique purpose to continue your work. In Jesus name, Amen.

Reflection

Do you know what your purpose is?

Why are you in pursuit of purpose?

Have you gotten discouraged in your quest for purpose? If so, Why?

How will knowing your purpose make an impact in your life?

Faith Confession

I am sincerely seeking God's purpose for my life. I understand that my purpose here on earth is ultimately to fulfill the will of God.

DAY 16

Conversations with God

How you view and understand God determines how you communicate with Him.

"I love God, but God and I don't talk like that anymore." This was a phrase from a woman in the audience on Oprah's Life Class. She stood up to speak about moving past hurt and not feeling good about herself. Her statement was very interesting but not surprising. Can you identify with this woman? Do you desire to discover your purpose but you aren't talking to God? Some may say, "How can you say you love God but you don't talk to him?" It is actually very easy. Loving God and communing with Him are two different things but, yet, dependent on each other. You can love God out of obligation because of what He has done or because you know it is the right thing to do, but never have a pure personal love relationship with Him. He wants to tell you all about you just like Jesus did for the woman at the well. The Bible tells the story of a Samaritan woman who went about her normal routine to draw water from the well when she encountered and had a conversation with Jesus. He tells her all about herself, things that no one else would know. She was so amazed that she went into the town telling everyone about Him. Do you want that amazing experience? Are you thirsty for more of God? Your quest for purpose will place you in a posture to commune with God on a deeper level. It will teach you how to come into fellowship with Him through the purity of your heart. The dynamics of your relationship with God has to change from no longer being from a surface place but from a deep and sincere place. It is important that you remove the walls, barriers, the familiar, and your intellect so you can communicate with Him. Do whatever it takes to get into that still, quiet, and peaceful place so He can minister to you. He wants to take you on a journey and reveal new things. He desires for you to meet truth that your worship, praise, and thanksgiving comes from your spirit. There is no need to be intimidated but rather be free to release it all in prayer. God wants you to release it all so He can give you true fulfillment. Some of you may say, "I don't know how to pray." Just talk to your father and tell Him how you feel and what you desire. Prayer and time with God is not meant to make you feel unqualified or incapable but it is for you to communicate and experience the sweet gentle loving spirit of your father. Take time and commune with God because it is your lifeline, it is what brings clarity, and it is where your receive answers. It is your weapon against the enemy.

Today, I challenge you to spend time meditating, praying, and communicating with God. Stay sensitive to His voice and be comforted today. Read the word of God and keep your ears open to hear.

Daily Scripture
"GOD's there, listening for all who pray,
for all who pray and mean it."
(Psalm 145:18 MSG)

Prayer
Father, I thank you for desiring to commune with me. I thank you that I can come to you in prayer and release and receive. You are such a loving father who loves me in spite of. Thank you for leading and guiding me into all truth. In Jesus name, Amen.

Reflections
Do you need to commune with God?

Spend at least an extra 30 minutes dedicated to prayer and reading God's word.

Journal your experience.

Faith Confession
I will make a decision to open up and allow God into the deep places of my heart. I will no longer approach Him from a surface level but from the deep places within me.

DAY 17

Consistency

True consistency happens when you are in a place of total focus, faith, and confidence.

I have learned that consistency is key to success and it is one of the areas while many of us fall short. Whether it is consistency in how you discipline your children, consistency in exercising, or consistency in prayer. You will not be able to achieve your desired results without it. It is the same with your quest for purpose. Ladies, you have to be consistent in your seek and not allow emotions to cause inconsistency. You can't be on fire to discover your purpose today and then tomorrow you are down in your emotions and you forget all about it. If you do not deal with your emotions, it will cause you to be inconsistent and lose the intensity that you once had. God honors your perseverance. Giving up is not an option. Instead, I encourage you to find out what is taking your focus, faith, and confidence. You must deal with those issues or they will make an appearance in every area of your life. Are you really ready to seek after God's purpose for your life until it is revealed? I promise you that each day will reveal more of your purpose. I have learned that purpose evolves. What you know today about your purpose may just be a glimpse of what is to come. As you flow in your purpose, it will evolve and reveal new things. Yes, distractions will come, but stay focused. If you get off track make sure you pick back up as soon as possible and keep pressing. No matter what the circumstances are, you owe it to yourself to stay committed to what you are in search of. When you are consistent, you will increase in discipline, patience, endurance, clarity, and confidence.

Today, I want you to make a decision to be consistent. Get rid of those bad habits that invite inconsistency in your life like self-sabotaging thoughts, procrastination, and laziness. So let me ask you a question…How bad do you want it?

Daily Scripture
"You will seek me and find me when you seek me with all your heart."
(Jeremiah 29:13 NIV)

Prayer
Father, I thank you for revealing to me the necessity of consistency. Thank you for being patient with me as I grow in commitment and discipline. Teach me how to stay focused to the task that is before me that I would accomplish everything you have called me to. In Jesus name, Amen.

Reflection
Have you been consistent with your quest for purpose?

What barriers keep you from being consistent and seeing results in your life?

What are ways you can boost the level of consistency as you seek your purpose?

Faith Confession
Today, I make a commitment to be consistent. I will remove all barriers and distractions and stay focused no matter what. I will see results in my life.

DAY 18

Obedience

My desire is not to take anything away from you but to increase you even the more. Your obedience is tied to your trust and love for me. Don't fall into a position where I need to extend grace unnecessarily. Just be obedient and follow me. (This is what the Lord says)

Do you hear God speaking? Has He given you instructions? Has He told you to disconnect yourself from something or someone that you are still connected to? God is expecting you to be obedient. He has given us all a promise but our obedience will determine if we receive the fullness of it. When you are obedient to just one instruction there are so many rewards and benefits that can come out of it. Oftentimes the struggle in obedience is a lack of trust, fear, the issue of disciplining our flesh, and letting go of control. Yes, you are great, intelligent and strong, but God is all knowing and He needs to be in control of your life. You can no longer navigate through life constantly attempting to control the destinations and outcomes. It will only delay your divine destiny and invite frustration. I had to learn this the hard way. I did not know how to let God totally be in control of my life. So He placed me in a situation that caused me to surrender my will and control and take on His will for my life. It was a painful process yet liberating to my spirit. I was finally free of the responsibility of navigating my life and looking ahead to figure out my future. I finally understood that my future lies in God, and if I put my trust in Him and walk in obedience that it is His responsibility to order my steps. As you are on your quest for purpose, you will learn that obedience is necessary. Did I say it was easy? No, although it probably should be. After all, God knows what is best for you. One thing is for sure, you must make up in your mind to be obedient and follow the Lord as He guides you through discovering and walking in your purpose.

Disobedience will cost you. It will cost you time, joy, peace, money and true happiness.

Today, I want you to become aware of what causes you to walk in disobedience. It is important that you recognize the necessity of obedience and start today!

Daily Scripture
"Then Samuel said, Do you think all GOD wants are sacrifices— empty rituals just for show? He wants you to listen to him! Plain listening is the thing, not staging a lavish religious production.
Not doing what GOD tells you is far worse than fooling around in the occult. Getting self-important around GOD is far worse than making deals with your dead ancestors. Because you said No to GOD's command, he says No to your kingship."
(1 Samuel 15:22-23)

Prayer
Father, I thank you for extending grace to me even when I was disobedient. I thank you for showing me the importance of obedience and teaching me how to follow you no matter what. I will walk in obedience in Jesus name, Amen.

Reflection
In your quest for purpose, have you been obedient to God?

Do you struggle with obedience? Why?

How can you do better as it relates to obedience?

Faith Confession

I am going to make a commitment to be obedient to God. I understand that my obedience is critical to my destiny. It does not please God when I am disobedient. I am so grateful that he still gives me another chance.

DAY 19

Relationships

When God removes the superficial in you, you begin to look past the superficial in others to see their spirit. That is when the real relationship begins.

Relationships were designed to be a part of all of our lives. I believe that we were created to be in relationship with one another. How we relate and who we relate to is a mirror image of how we view ourselves. As God begins to shed you of those superficial things in your life, you will view relationships from a different perspective. Relationships were not meant to validate, complete you, define you, or make you happy. However, there is a purpose for every relationship both good and bad. Many of us feel lonely and we try and fill the void with what we believe are meaningful relationships when we really need to be filled with the love of God. As you go on a journey of discovery and embrace your purpose, your relationships will change. You will have to evaluate your friendships and put them in their proper place. Whether it is a relationship with your boyfriend, husband, Pastor, friends, family or business partner, all of them are meant to add value to your life and be supportive as you walk in purpose. Any connection with individuals who stifle you, bring doubt and fear into your life or cause you to compromise, need to be cut off. That is it and that is all. No negotiating! You have a right to love certain individuals from a distance and choose who is in your space. When God disconnects you from certain individuals don't pray for them to stay, but let them go so you will be free to receive what is next for you.

As you walk out purpose, God will send people to challenge you and cause you to dig deeper into yourself to discover more and to reach your full potential. Don't reject them but give room for growth to overtake you. You want to surround yourself with those that are going or are already where you know you will be. While in your journey, remember to look past the superficial and look at the spirit of the individual. Let me warn you, do not be distracted by the counterfeits. In other words, do not allow the enemy to distract you by sending people who were never meant to be in relationship with you. Relationships are vital to fulfilling your purpose. Be careful not to isolate yourself from the relationships that were sent to support you. As you are spinning and turning and being shaped, pressed and molded, be very careful of forming new relationships because once you become the new you, you may see people from a different lens.

Today, I want you to be aware of your relationships and evaluate them. Pray and ask God to show you if they are meant for this season of your life. You must become aware of how you relate with yourself. You must never allow a relationship to steal your authenticity-molding you into something that God never intended you to be.

Daily Scripture
"Become wise by walking with the wise; hang out with fools and watch your life fall to pieces."
(Proverbs 13:20 MSG)

Prayer
Father, I am grateful for the relationship that I have with you that has taught me how to relate to others. Thank you for favoring me with the gift of discernment on who to connect with and who to disconnect from. Continue to send those who are there to strengthen me and encourage me along the way. In Jesus name, Amen.

Reflection
Do you need to re-evaluate some of the relationships in your life?

Do an inventory of those persons who are in your space and determine if they add value to your life. Have you placed some people with the wrong priority?

Do you look for relationships to define who you are and to bring you happiness? Why?

Do you shy away from relationships? Why? It is very important to have healthy relationships. If you do not, what can you do to develop healthy relationships with others?

Faith Confession
Today, I understand that relationships are an essential part of my life. However, I will pray for an increase in discernment that I will not enter into relationships with people that God did not ordain for my life. I make a decision to disconnect from every person that doesn't belong in my life. I decree healthy relationships

DAY 20

The Awakening

This is not the time to sleep but to wake up, agree with God, and move!

Life is truly a beautiful journey and we discover something new about ourselves every day. In life you will encounter situations and circumstances that may push you into a dark and unfamiliar place. Have you ever been in that place called "stuck"? You love God, you desire to walk in purpose, you desire to pursue your dreams and your passion and to experience joy but, somewhere along your journey, you lost the light. You pray, you cry, you read the word of God, you seek advice from others and nothing seems to work. Unfortunately, nothing seems to get you out of that dream like state. I understand because I have been there. It is not an easy season to walk through but, eventually, it will work for your good. Sometimes that dream-like state is a defense mechanism and a way to cope with your disappointment in yourself; however, I believe that the spirit of awakening has come to you today!

An awakening is when you experience a connection with Holy Spirit and you come into the knowledge of yourself. You wake up! It is the moment when things come into alignment at the right time and you finally get it. What you have searched for has been there all along. It is like a breath of fresh air; you exhale and a door full of possibilities is opened before you. Ah, an awakening, what a great defining moment! All your gifts, talents, and desires have all been clues and catalysts leading you to discover your purpose. It all makes sense now. The reason that you are passionate about X; The reason that you desire Z; The reason that you are gifted in this particular area. It is all a part of your divine purpose. Yes, that special thing that you always envisioned yourself to be but never believed it was attainable, is now your divine purpose. Amazing! You have been walking with this precious gift all along. There are no coincidences in God. Every step that we take is ordered and is leading us to discover and fulfill what has already been planned for us.

Today, I want you to embrace the spirit of awakening and believe that you have already overcome! It is time that you awaken from your state of sleep and grab a hold to your purposed-filled life.

Daily Scripture

"For the light makes everything visible. This is why it is said, "Awake, O sleeper, rise up from the dead, and Christ will give you light.""
(Ephesians 5:14 NLT)

Prayer

Father, I thank you for allowing me to wake up. Thank you for sending the spirit of awakening into my life. Give me the endurance and the stamina needed to continue to walk in the light and become all that you have called me to be. I give you praise because I understand that my life has already made a change for the better. In Jesus name, Amen.

Reflection

What are your gifts and talents? How have you been using them?

What do you believe your purpose is?

Faith Confession
Today, I allow God's spirit to refresh, renew, and rest in
my spirit that I will wake up, become spiritually alert, and
get moving, quickly!

DAY 21

Forward March!

There will be no positioning, recovery, and promotion if you don't move.

Are you sitting at a yellow light moving with caution and waiting to go? Are you standing in front of a door waiting for it to open? Are you waiting for the finances to appear in your bank account before you move on your vision? Well my sister, God says, "Don't wait, MOVE FORWARD!" It is time to go forward in purpose. You must have no more doubt, no more fear, no more analyzing, no more looking for others to agree, just go. As one who is a planner, analyzer, and sometimes said to be a creature of habit, I am too familiar with not moving forward because of fear of the unknown. But there comes a time when you mature to a place where you throw caution to the wind, you stop worrying about all the details, you trust God for real, and you move forward; for remaining stagnant and going around in circles will not help you in gaining new territory. You will most likely end up complaining about what is not right in your life when the solution is in your movement. Yes, there is healing in your movement and even clarity comes when you are moving. You must not look for road signs, landmarks, or crossing guards, just move forward and God will be your navigation system. It is funny because oftentimes we wait to hear the answers from God when His answer is simply GO! When you start moving, He will start directing you because your steps are already ordered. If you recall in the Bible whenever Jesus healed someone He said, "Go in peace, Go and sin no more." There is power when you move. You evolve in purpose not by standing still but by moving forward. Sometimes we can be so overwhelmed with hurt, disappointment, worry, and stress that we can't even think about moving forward. These stumbling blocks keep you from moving forward with your assignment. As you go forward, you will be walking out purpose and moving further and further away from what once hindered you. Today, don't procrastinate, it is time for you to move forward. Make up in your mind that you will progress in purpose.

Daily Scripture
"But Jesus told him, "anyone who puts a hand to the plow and then looks back is not fit for the kingdom of God.""
(Luke 9:62 NLT)

Prayer
Father, I pray that you would empower me to move forward in everything that you have called me to do. I ask that you would teach me how to disconnect from procrastination to move forward without delay. I thank you that you have been patient with me as I get it right. I trust you and I know that you know exactly what is ahead of me. Teach me to move forward without fear knowing that I am able to conquer all that is before me. In Jesus name, Amen.

Reflection
What is stopping you from taking the steps to go forward?

Are you really ready and committed to following God and walking in your purpose?

Faith Confession
Today, I declare that I will go forward regardless of what appears to be a stumbling block. I will stand tall and move forward.

CELEBRATE YOURSELF!

Congratulations! You have now completed 21 days. It is the ending of three seven day cycles. You are halfway there to the new you! Do something special for yourself today and enjoy walking in purpose! You are one step closer to becoming the New You! It's a revolution!

WEEK FOUR

The Art of Becoming

It is the stretching, the pressing, the relinquishing of self, and the willingness to embrace your process that will prepare you for the next phase of your life.

It is always amazing to me to think of the metamorphosis of a caterpillar. How something not so beautiful evolves into something very beautiful. This wonderful process by which a caterpillar morphs into a butterfly may not be comfortable, but it is necessary for the transformation. It will never fly if it aborts its natural process of development. This process happens in our lives. As you surrender to God's plan, experience more of life, and apply lessons that you have learned, a new person emerges. I believe it is necessary to appreciate every part of your journey to becoming who God has called you to be. The new you is not something you can "fake until you make it", it is not something you can be until you become.

Many individuals are trying to **be** before they **become**. No one can teach you how to become; it has to be lived and experienced. Pain, misunderstanding, hurt, fear, rejection, the unknown, it is all a part of your process to becoming. God has a specific path designed for you and how you navigate through it is shaping and developing you. It is imperative to stay in the flow of God for your life. While you are evolving, you cannot focus on what others are doing around you. Just allow God to mold you into your authentic self. As you become who God has ordained you to be, your perspective will change, your faith will be strengthened, and you will build your confidence. Evolution brings about new understanding, knowledge, and passion.

This week I want you to tap into becoming who God has ordained you to be. Please do not discredit your days of weeping, questions, frustration, and confusion. It is intricately working together to shift you, rechannel your thoughts, and to birth a new level of awareness. Our upcoming topics involve: Renewing Your Mind; Your Wealthy Place; Surrender & Flow; Faith; Transition; Decisions; and Reinvent Yourself. It is your time to become the new you. Don't fight the process! It is not as hard as you think!

DAY 22

Renew Your Mind

—————————————✳—————————————

*The filters of your mind are being purified. Arise, be filled &
flourish.*

"For as he thinks in his heart so is he."(Proverbs 23:7

AMP) I love this scripture because it is so simple but

invokes us to really evaluate our thought process on a

deeper level. Whatever you think is what you believe and

what you believe is what you speak, and what you speak is

what you will have. The "new you" requires that you renew

your mind so your life will be transformed. You have to

believe the word that God has spoken over your life. How

do you see yourself? Is it how God sees you? How do you

view your business? Is it how God views it? You must

renew your mind by reading the word of God daily so that

the truth is revealed unto you. Then it is your responsibility

to put it into action so you may receive God's promises for

your life. Change your perspective. Don't look at the situation as a road block but an opportunity to creatively solve a problem. Approach your journey from a positive place, change your focus, and believe that all things are possible. Along with changing your focus comes the need for truth. Renewing your mind will cause you to open up to new ideas and truths that will alter your belief system and thrust you into a new level of consciousness. Every day you should want to renew your mind that you are able to embrace what God wants to do in your life in the present not the past. The past is the past, you must leave it there. When your mind is renewed you are able to enjoy the moment and await your future.

Today, I want you to seek after new revelation and understanding. Unlock the shallow places in your mind and soar to new heights. Meditate on the word of God and allow it to find a resting place in your heart.

Daily Scripture
"Therefore, I urge you, brothers and sisters, in view of God's mercy, to offer your bodies as a living sacrifice, holy and pleasing to God—this is your true and proper worship. Do not conform to the pattern of this world, but be transformed by the renewing of your mind. Then you will be able to test and approve what God's will is—his good, pleasing and perfect will."
(Romans 12:1-2 NIV)

Prayer
Father, I ask you to take my mind and transform it. Give me a renewed mind that I increase in the things of you. In Jesus name, Amen.

Reflection
What are three ways that you can renew your mind?

Are you afraid of change? Why?

What are you most excited about as it relates to becoming the new you?

Faith Confession
Today, I commit to the process of renewing my mind so I can become all that God has destined me to be. Old thinking is out the window and I invite God in to channel my mind on a different frequency.

DAY 23

Your Wealthy Place

The pain may be great. The attack may be difficult to bear but God is greater. You will prevail. You will produce. You will arrive at your wealthy place.

Who wants to feel pain, hurt and experience suffering? I don't believe that any of us willingly want to go through, what I call, the fire. But I have learned that it is absolutely necessary for your growth and development and becoming your expected end. Many of you desire to be wealthy in that you are whole in every area of your life. Your wealthy place, your place of abundance and prosperity comes through affliction. I can testify that whenever my life was shifting to another dimension there was always a time of affliction, trial, and pruning. It certainly doesn't feel good, but at the same time you are able to see the hand of God in the midst. It is something about the fire that prunes you, purifies you, and shows you what you are really made of.

Your appreciation and love for God will increase by leaps and bounds. The way you view yourself, your life, and others will shift. Understand that your wealthy place is not about money, clothes, houses, and cars but it has everything to do with your ability to produce tangible things from the womb of your spirit. What do I mean by that? Once you grow spiritually and become more of who God desires you to be, you will be able to flow with Him in a realm where whatever you speak has to manifest because you are connected to His will for your life. An individual can be wealthy and live in a one bedroom apartment. It is not about the natural but the spirit. Whatever you produce in the spirit has to come to pass in the natural. It is the law of reciprocity. What you put into the atmosphere is what you will receive in return. Affliction fortifies you in strength. It increases you in wisdom, power, and authority. It refines you to the place that you stand in purpose and press forward in the midst of adversity because you recognize who lives inside of you. Your wealthy place is birthed

through affliction and it is definitely a part of the process of

becoming.

Today, I want you to embrace the difficult moments in

your life. Be thankful for your affliction and recognize it as

the vehicle to your place of true abundance.

Daily Scripture
"For you, God, tested us; you refined us like silver. You
brought us into prison and laid burdens on our backs. You
let people ride over our heads; we went through fire and
water, but you brought us to a place of abundance."
(Psalm 66:10-12 NIV)

Prayer
Father, I thank you for showing me that you did not send
the affliction to harm or destroy me but to make me better.
I understand that my ways are not like your ways and you
do all things well. Thank you for pruning me and
performing a work inside me that I may be the fulfillment
of your word. In Jesus name, Amen.

Reflection
Are you angry at God for what you have or are enduring
right now?

Have you viewed your affliction as something sent to
destroy you?

After reading today, do you now see how your afflictions were sent to work for your good?

Faith Confession
Today, I release any anger or bitterness I have been harboring because of my affliction. I now understand that it is working for my good.

DAY 24

Surrender & Flow

Release and surrender yourself to the will of God. Recognize that you are not in control.

How many of you truly want to live a purposed-filled life of peace, joy, and love? This kind of life is attainable when you make a decision to flow with God. I am not saying that you will be exempt from trials and turbulent times. But your ability to be tenacious and navigate through them all, will be enhanced. You cannot flow with God until you surrender. It is like traveling on a road trip. You cannot put your car on cruise control until you have achieved a certain speed. Agreeing with God and the word that He has spoken over your life and surrendering to His will for your life, are prerequisites to truly flowing with Him. Do you want what God wants for your life or do you want what God never intended for your life? When you surrender, what you are saying is that you accept His will for your life and anything that doesn't line up with that you will not allow in your life. Don't tie God's hands, but allow Him to freely flow in your life. To agree just doesn't involve a confession with your mouth but it must be coupled with focused, intentional, and purposed driven actions. You cannot say that you are in agreement with God when it comes to your relationships and continue to co-mingle with individuals that compromise your worth and your wealth. Instead, be intentional about the choices you make as an outward expression of surrendering to God.

When you move in sync with God, surrender and let go of the control, you will soar to higher heights. There is also a certain order that needs to be present in your life so you can properly flow with God. The good news is that once you make a decision, order will begin to align itself as you move. Sometimes it comes in the form of instructions and other times it comes in the form of strategy. You see, the bottom line is that your freedom depends on your surrender. He has given you the freedom to be, so what better time to flow! Stay in prayer, stay in worship, stay in expectation of what is to come. This is the time to keep your eyes open and your ears sensitive to the voice of God and move when He tells you to move. You don't want distraction to intervene with your flow. Just as rivers flow into one major body of water, so will everything in your life flow into the flow of God creating an overflow of manifested blessings. Today, I want you to agree with God, relinquish control, surrender and flow.

Daily Scripture
"He who believes in Me[who cleaves to and trusts in and relies on Me] as the Scripture has said, From his innermost being shall flow [continuously] springs and rivers of living water."
(John 7:38 AMP)

Prayer
Father, I thank you for teaching me how to flow with you. I ask that you be my guide and speak to me along the way.

Make it plain to me that I would not be distracted and that I make it to the place of overflow. In Jesus name, Amen.

Reflection
Let's do a *flow* check.

Are you still trying to guide your own life?

Have you let go of the reigns and let God be God?

Are you moving into the direction that God is flowing?

What areas in your life need order?

How can you create more order in your life?

Faith Confession
Today, I make a commitment to place things in my life in proper priority. I will increase the flow of order in my life. I am free, and I will flow with God and receive every blessing that He has for me! Whatever doesn't fit into the flow of God for my life, I release it today.

DAY 25

Faith

Just because you don't see it doesn't mean it is not there. Choose to believe.

Have you tried to figure it out? Have you tried to create a strategy or a plan? Have you said to yourself, "Well I am going to give it to God and let Him handle it?" Meanwhile, you continue to have your hands in it? Do you want to see the evidence before you believe the outcome? I have done it all and let me tell you that is not faith in God, but belief in our own abilities, which are finite, unless we connect to the faith we have in God. Faith is not about what you see in the natural but what you don't see in the natural but see and believe in the spirit. "Now faith is the substance of things hoped for, the evidence of things not seen."(Hebrews 11:1KJV) Faith is your evidence and it says that what is not seen will soon be visible. Faith is not reactive but it is proactive. It is not predicated upon your circumstances but faith stands as the evidence and the reality which keeps your circumstances, from having power.

As you become and evolve, God will send you on a faith walk. I have been in the place where it didn't seem like the right time, money was not plentiful, nothing about the situation seemed right but God said yes. The journey to becoming has everything to do with stretching your faith to receive what has already been established by God. I speak to you my sister, the one with a dream but fear has told you to wait. I speak to you my sister, the one who has wavered in her faith due to transition and difficult trials. It is time to open up your spirit and let faith be your voice. God gave you the precious gift of faith; make Him proud and work your faith. Faith without works is dead. Release your faith and couple it with your actions and you are sure to have a divine explosion! Your faith is not dead because it is very much alive. I learned that walking in faith is not about being perfect, but your willingness to please God through the exercising of your faith.

Today, I challenge you to let go of fear, trust God and believe that He will do exactly what He said He would do. Live again and walk in faith. I challenge you to think of the thing that you have thought was impossible, confess the word of God, and put your faith on it.

Daily Scripture
"But without faith it is impossible to please him: for he that cometh to God must believe that he is, and he is a rewarder of them that diligently seek him."
(Hebrews 11:6 KJV)

Prayer
Father, I thank you for the gift of faith. I pray that where my faith has wavered that you would restore it. I ask that you teach me how to release my faith and believe that whatever I need is already done. I pray that you send opportunities for my faith to be strengthened and exercised. In Jesus name, Amen.

Reflection
Are you wavering in Faith? Why?

What do you believe God for? Do you have faith that He will bring it to pass?

I challenge you to create a faith box. Every day I want you to write your faith requests, confess it, and place it in the box. Believe and have faith that they will come to pass.

Faith Confession
Today, I let go of fear and I release my faith. I trust God and I believe that He will do what He said. I may not see it in the natural, but I believe by faith that it has already happened.

DAY 26

Transition

It is through the uncertainty of transition that you are redirected, stabilized, and fortified.

How did I get here? Nothing looks familiar. Wait, I'm not ready to deal with this yet. Do these words sound familiar? When it is your time to transition to a greater destination, God will allow you to be right in the middle of a place called, "What the Heck is this!" You are traveling through life maintaining, content, comfortable, and then out of nowhere something hits your life and BAM...changes everything! How do you handle it? What do you do? Well, you embrace it, you cry through it, you grow through it, you live through it and become the new you!

Whether you know it or not your life is constantly moving and shifting. God has you on a divine schedule and it is leading you to your destiny. As you mature in your spiritual walk and evolve in purpose, you will experience

multiple seasons of transition each bringing a different trial,

experience, and revelation. As you become, transition is

eminent. If you feel somewhat off balance, emotionally

challenged and lonely, even when people are

around…don't panic, it is a normal part of transition. God

is stretching you, pruning you, equipping you, and shifting

you to your next dimension in Him. Allow the process to

work. Transition is quite uncomfortable as it feels like you

are in outer space between two destinations. You are not

where you were and you are not where you are going. Be

encouraged as this is only a temporary position and it is

rewarding and it is necessary. Stay sensitive to the voice of

God and only move as He directs you. Don't give up, but

pray for the endurance to keep moving.

Today, I want you to know that your place of "old" has

served its purpose in your life and God is now renewing

you, shifting you, and increasing your capacity for your next. Be encouraged today, you are not crazy, you are not out of His will; you are in transition! I want you to take a moment to reflect on where you were and where you are now and journal your thoughts, new revelations, and what you see in your future.

Daily Scripture
"Have I not commanded you? Be strong and courageous. Do not be afraid; do not be discouraged, for the LORD your God will be with you wherever you go."
(Joshua 1:9 NIV)

Prayer
Father, I thank you for the time of transition. I understand that it serves a purpose in my life. When it comes, help me to stand strong and to keep moving. Help me to stay sensitive to your voice so I know which path I should take. In Jesus name, Amen.

Reflection
Are you in transition? How do you feel? How are you coping?

What have you learned? What are you committed to improving?

Faith Confession

Today, I understand that transition is all a part of the process to becoming and is necessary for my spiritual maturity. I submit to the will of God for my life, and I believe that He is guiding my every step.

Decision

There is a difference between a decision and direction. God is waiting on you to make a decision so He can give you direction.

Throughout my life, I often heard, "just make a decision!" On my best day, I can be the poster child of indecisiveness. I am one that sees the good side and the bad side. I weighed all my options first so making a decision was a daunting task until I began to realize the reason behind my indecisiveness. Can you guess? It was fear, control, and uncertainty. So during my transition, I had to let God deal with that part of me. I found that making decisions are crucial to your future. I remember praying and pleading with God to tell me what to do and He gave me the revelation that He was waiting on me to make a decision so He could give me direction; that blew my mind. God is so awesome that He gave us power and authority to make our own way prosperous. He gave us the tools we need to be successful and accomplish what He called us to do. While you are becoming, God will place you in predicaments that will call for you to make a decision. Please do not run away from it but embrace it. He is elevating you to a new level of power and authority in Him, the question is, can you handle it?

One of the key factors that can affect our decisions is our emotions. We as women are known for being emotional creatures. Some of us are better than others but, at some point in time, we have all ended up in a mess led by our emotions. Your emotions and issues will ultimately affect your decisions and that is a recipe for disaster. It is important that you deal with them so you can make wise and purposed decisions. If you have been making decisions without the leading of Holy Spirit a change needs to take place. Although we have the power to choose, it does not cancel the need to pray before making those choices. Many of you may end up in bad relationships, dead end jobs, churches where you don't belong all because you failed to consult God before making a decision. Some of you need to make decisions to move forward and advance no matter the cost. Some of you need to make a decision to leave your past, a toxic relationship, or unfruitful habits. Your journey to becoming involves making tough but necessary decisions. Your destiny is shaped by the decisions and choices you make. God is waiting to direct you but you have to first make a decision.

Today, I want you to focus on the decisions that you need to make right now. You should not go into the next month or the next year without having made those necessary decisions that will shape your divine future.

Daily Scripture
"Without counsel purposes are disappointed: but in the multitude of counselors they are established."
(Proverbs 15:22KJV)

Prayer
Father, I thank you for giving me discernment to make decisions. I thank you for directing my path. I will follow wherever you lead me. In Jesus name, Amen.

Reflection
What decisions do you need to make? What can you do to make your decision process easier?

What decisions have you made that you didn't seek the counsel of Holy Spirit? What did you learn from it?

Some of you may struggle with making decisions because you don't trust yourself or you are afraid to make the wrong decision. If this is you, I challenge you to do something different. Don't look for others to agree with or validate your decisions. Trust yourself.

Faith Confession
Today, I make the decisions to release my past, trust God and move forward. Whenever the need for decision arises, I will consult Holy Spirit for guidance and then I will make a wise decision.

DAY 28

Reinvent Yourself

Don't fight it. Don't intellectualize it. Don't smother it. Now is the time for the real you to emerge.

Have you ever felt amazingly different, but weird all at the same time? Perhaps you can't put your finger on it, but you know that something new and great is on the horizon. I remember sitting by the water shortly after I had just separated from my husband and tears were flowing and the Lord spoke to me and said, "I'm going to teach you how to reinvent yourself." Immediately I knew that my life wasn't over and my destiny had not been destroyed. In fact, it was the beginning of the new me. Just as those words encouraged me, I believe they will do the same for you. It is time to reinvent yourself. It is time to upgrade your thinking and adjust the dynamics of how you *"do you"*. Just as a company develops new strategies and rebrands itself as it evolves, God desires to teach you how to become a polished and refreshed you. Nobody can be you, but you! Whatever you are experiencing right now that challenges the very essence of you, take your focus off of it and believe that the value of your brand is getting ready to increase because of it. Reinvent yourself!

There are some trials that come into our life that will literally knock us to the ground. It can feel as though life as you know it will never be the same again. I encourage you to take those remnants of hope, joy and strength that are left and reinvent yourself. You have everything you need to rebuild. It is in these times that God makes you aware of what you didn't know was there. Sometimes it takes a life altering situation to make you resilient. Remove what drains you, refocus your mind, assess yourself, and grab a hold to your greatest asset for you haven't lost anything except what needed to go! It is not too late. It is time to get a new lease on life. It can be as simple as breaking habits and routines, trying new things and becoming more resourceful. Reinventing yourself is simply a divine transformation by way of divine inspiration. Be inspired to live again. Open up your spirit and receive the fresh wind of new possibilities and opportunities. I challenge you to take the limits off and soar. Let your hair down, buy a new pair of shoes, try a new shade of lipstick. Girl, live and laugh again! The new you is emerging.

Today I want you to allow God to show you how to reinvent yourself. I believe resurgence has hit your life and you will never be the same. Let Him upgrade you!

Daily Scripture
"But forget all that – it is nothing compared to what I am going to do. For I am about to do something new. See, I have already begun! Do you not see it? I will make a pathway through the wilderness through the wilderness. I will create rivers in the dry wasteland."
(Isaiah 43:18-19NLT)

Prayer

Father, I thank you for new life in you. I thank you that regardless of what I have been through that a refreshing is headed my way. I pray that you would teach me how to reinvent myself and how to be resilient. I know that all things are working together for my good. I pray that you remove all worry and anxiety about what is ahead of me and you give me peace. In Jesus name, Amen.

Reflection

When you envision the ideal **you** what do you see? Do you believe that what you see can become a reality?

What can you do to assist in reinventing yourself?

I am all about names and slogans. They are powerful and speak volumes. Just for fun. I want you to write your name and then come up with a tagline that defines the new you.
Example:
Latoya A. Benson - No delay, No limits, No fear

Faith Confession

Today, I decree and declare that my change is already here. I recognize and understand that my destiny is not destroyed or delayed. I will bounce back, reinvent myself, and recover all. A spiritual makeover has taken place and my official launch date is right around the corner.

CELEBRATE YOURSELF!

Congratulations! You have completed week four of your 40 day journey. So it's that time again…it is time to celebrate. You are on your way to becoming the New You! It's a revolution!

WEEK FIVE

The Freedom to Be!

Freedom can be instantaneous if you embrace it.

The chains have been broken, restoration has come, and the door has been opened. Will you seize this opportunity to soar as an eagle? Freedom is a gift but it is up to you to choose to receive it. Jesus is Freedom. He came to set the captives free, He came to free us from the bondage of religion and tradition. He came to release you into the beauty of freedom. In case you didn't know, you have been given the freedom to be. Are you still bound by the chains of yesterday? In order to be free, you must embrace the God of TODAY. Your past and freedom have nothing in common. No more apologies for being who you are. No more compromising to fit into society's mold. God created you to be that pink elephant in the room so STAND OUT!

As you progress in your journey, there is a mindset you enter into that feels like childhood all over again. You feel free, uninhibited, fearless, and ready to conquer whatever comes your way. You are free to be! When this happens, you have tapped into the assurance of the gift giver. You, my sister have no more excuses. He has given you the freedom to be exactly who He called you to be. You are free and you are in control of your destiny by the steps you take and the actions you make. Don't stay in bondage because you refuse to open your mind to the new. You have been given permission to sing a new song, dance a new dance, and live through purpose. This week you will focus on the topics: Believe in Yourself; No Fear; Success is Yours; Rest in HIM; Speak It; Imagine Me – Above and Beyond and A Woman of Influence. Don't delay another minute, your freedom awaits.

DAY 29

Believe in Yourself

Deep inside you know exactly what you possess and its worth. Trust it.

Have you ever had an idea such as a business, event, gathering, or a dream vacation and you didn't follow through because of doubt? I have, and I came to the conclusion that it wasn't God's inability to bring it to pass, I simply did not believe in myself. It is difficult for others to believe in you if you don't first believe in yourself. More importantly, you are the fulfillment of God's plan over your life and if you don't believe in yourself, you impede the joy in walking out the plan. Always questioning, doubting, and wavering will leave you stagnant.

To believe in yourself says you stand in confidence of what you possess. It says that regardless of those who don't agree with you that you have enough confidence in yourself to keep moving. I have struggled with self-confidence. I would place my confidence and belief in someone else's abilities before my own. It was interesting to see how God removed those people out of my life so I would learn to be confident in myself. When you believe in yourself and stand in Godly confidence, there is nothing you can't accomplish. You will increase in boldness and authority and stand sure-footed with a focused mind. God's word is what we can count on to increase our belief in ourselves and build our self-confidence. If you are reading this and you say to yourself, "I am already confident." I congratulate you and challenge you to continuing growing. For others, I challenge you to search your heart and be sure that you are not operating in false confidence. On the outside, you are as bold as a lion but on the inside there is someone who needs to connect to something real.

Today, I empower you to believe in yourself. Be

confident in who you are and what you do. Continue to

receive knowledge, wisdom and understanding and read

God's word for assurance. I encourage you today to be

confident in what God is doing on the inside of you. The

more you become confident in God, the more you will

believe in yourself. You will only be as effective and

successful as you are confident.

Daily Scripture
"If you can? said Jesus, everything is possible for one who
believes."
(Mark 9:23NIV)
Read the full story Mark 9:14-29

Prayer
Father, I thank you for teaching me how to believe in
myself. Where there once was disbelief and doubt I now
walk in confidence believing that I shall have whatsoever I
say. Thank you, in Jesus name, Amen.

Reflection
Do you believe in yourself? Why or why not?

Are you always confident, even when trials or situations of
uncertainty arise?

If you waiver in your confidence, evaluate why and write a list of some ways you can increase in confidence and belief in yourself.

Faith Confession
I believe in myself because God believes in me. I am confident in myself because I am confident in the God I serve. All things are possible for me if I just believe. Today, I awaken my dreams, goals and ideas, and I believe I will succeed.

DAY 30

No Fear

A warrior doesn't walk in fear because he understands he is walking in authority.

She used to be a go-getter and a risk-taker. If you wanted to try something new and needed a partner, she was the one to call. But after a series of attempts at following her dreams and being rejected, her once "nothing can stop me" attitude began to slowly shrink. Now, it is like she is on vacation from being bold and ambitious. Do you know her? Her name is Miss Fear.

Fear, I know it all too well. It seems like out of nowhere it gripped me and wouldn't let me go. At first I thought it was only present in some areas of my life. However, in reality once fear found an open door it began to infiltrate my mind and affect every area of my life. Can you relate? Fear can manifest itself in so many ways; fear of the unknown, fear of succeeding, fear of failure, fear to trust, fear to let go. Fear is the exact opposite of faith and it can deter and delay you from becoming all God has called you to be. Fear is not an option in your journey to becoming.

As you evolve, God will place you in situations that require you to move past your fear and go after what is rightfully yours. If you are dealing with the stronghold of fear know that it is not from God. You have the power and authority to speak to it and overcome it. Do not let fear drive you away from your destiny. The time has come for you to face your fears and conquer them. There is a warrior within you that has been released for battle. There is no need to fear because God has already called you victorious. Do you trust God to take care of you? God has released you into your place of purpose and abundance. You must walk in it and embrace it. There is no room for fear.

Today, I want you to be honest with yourself and identity the root of your fear. It is time to give fear the boot and trust God.

Daily Scripture
"For God hath not given us the spirit of fear; but of power, and of love, and of a sound mind."
(2 Timothy 1:7 KJV)

Prayer
Father, I thank you for always being there for me. I pray that you would help me deal with my fears and overcome them. I understand that you have not given me the spirit of fear, so I ask that you show me how to stand in your power. You have already overcome every fear I could ever have so if I put my trust in you, there is nothing I can't do. In Jesus name, Amen.

Reflection
What are you afraid of?

Where did you first notice the spirit of fear being present in your life?

What practical steps can you take to overcoming your fears?

Faith Confession
I will no longer be afraid of what God has already equipped me to do. I will release my fears, walk in faith, and trust God. When I feel feelings of fear, I will make faith confessions and speak the word of God. I am victorious and an overcomer. In Jesus name, Amen.

DAY 31

Success is Yours

Do not despise small beginnings. The size of a thing does not determine its impact.

Society has a way of measuring one's success based on economic status, education, and material possessions. Some of us have been chasing a dream to meet society's standard and to accomplish our own need to be successful. In actuality, that is not true success but a false sense of fulfillment eventually leading to a bigger void. When you embrace the freedom to be, you understand that success is not based on man's measuring stick, agenda or calendar. Success is not based on connecting with cliques that seem to have it going on. Success says that you are accomplishing the plan, assignment, and purpose that God has for your life. Don't get me wrong, there is nothing wrong with wanting to be successful but do not allow the hype of success to overshadow the purpose for success. Unless you understand its purpose and are connected to God, success will just be an added responsibility that you are not equipped to handle.

You should be grateful that God has given you the freedom to be and through Him success is yours. No more comparing yourself to what the next person is doing. No more looking at where you live, what you drive, or what you wear and allowing it to define success in your life because none of this matters. Many of you may struggle with the woulda, coulda, shoulda blues that does nothing but stunt your growth and delay true success in your life. It is time to get up, be free, and create the success that God has already said is yours. Everything you have endured thus far is instrumental in your success.

Today, I want to empower you to think big, recognize that success is yours, pursue it, and be free. You were made for this.

Daily Scripture
"For promotion cometh neither from the east, nor from the west, nor from the south. But God is the judge: he putteth down one, and setteth up another."
(Psalm 75:6-7KJV)

Prayer
Father, I give you thanks and I am forever grateful that you have given me a life of success. I pray that you would keep me focused on my purpose and continue to make my crooked places straight. I ask that you send people into my life that I may be a blessing to. In Jesus name, Amen.

Reflection
What is your idea of success?

What steps have you taken to achieve success in your life?

If your success is based on your material possessions, where did that reasoning come from?

Faith Confession
Today, I understand that my success is not based on man's interpretation but fulfilling my God-given purpose. I was made for this and already destined to succeed. True success is mine!

DAY 32

Rest in HIM

What do you do when you don't know what to do? Just chill and rest in HIM.

Were we there when God spoke and framed the world? Are we responsible for waking ourselves up every morning? No; so it sounds to me like God has everything under control. So why do we worry, stress, and try to handle a job that we were never meant to handle? I remember when I was enduring so much that I let worry, stress, and anxiety creep into my life. I was sitting in my bedroom one day and I heard God say, Latoya just chill and rest in me. I immediately chuckled and smiled. I knew that God was reminding me that I was stepping out of bounds and walking into His territory. I was trying to be in control instead of relaxing and enjoying the benefits that come with me being a daughter of the King. There is no need to worry when He tells you to cast your cares on Him. All you need to do is chill and let God be God. If you begin to put this principle into operation, you will see that in the midst of being calm your answer will be there waiting. Either you will realize that it wasn't as bad as it looked or you will find peace in knowing that everything will be okay. And there is something very powerful that comes when you become calm. You will be able to exercise your God-given authority and power. When Daniel was thrown into the lions' den he remained calm and exercised his power and authority. He shut the mouths of the lions and they did not harm him.

Just when you start walking in your freedom, the spirit of stress can be released to push you into a state of panic, but don't let it take you off the course of resting in God. Sometimes we respond to people and situations when a response is not necessary. These types of situations are not worth your time or energy. Give it to God and let it go. You will experience situations that come into your life that are so much bigger than you and you have no choice but to trust God. You can't handle it, so why stress and worry over it. Don't panic but instead pray, give it to God, and just chill.

Today, I want you to remain calm and operate from a position of authority. No stress, no worry, no anxiety. It is already done. You just have to believe it. Rest in HIM.

Daily Scripture
"Do not be anxious about anything, but in every situation, by prayer and petition, with thanksgiving, present your requests to God."
(Philippians 4:6 NIV)

Prayer
Father, I thank you that you are a sovereignt God. I thank you that you are my protector. I am grateful that you have given me power over stress, worry, anxiety and any other spirits of oppression. I will give it all to you and rest knowing that you have it all under control. In Jesus name, Amen.

Reflection
Why is it so important for you to chill and rest?

Do you feel powerless when you aren't able to control situations?

If you are dealing with stress, worry and anxiety, what are some things you can do to counteract them?

Faith Confession
Today I free myself from every spirit of oppression. I will no longer be stressed, worried, or anxious about anything. I will operate in the freedom that God has given me. I am no longer bound but I am free.

DAY 33

Speak It

Your ability to speak is priceless. Remember, the atmosphere is producing what you speak.

So you really want me to believe that if I speak words out of my mouth things will change? Yea, right! Well, those were the words that I often said. I had experienced so much disappointment and rejection that I didn't believe that anything great would happen for me. I became content with what I was given and continued through life in silence. If you have ever been disappointed, rejected, or experienced a major loss then you probably understand what I mean. I had inadvertently gave away one of the most important things we have as believers, and that is our ability to speak. When God has given you the freedom to be, the best thing you can do is speak. Your desired outcome will be achieved when you speak with power and authority and believe what you speak. The more you speak, the more you will believe.

The New You won't emerge if you don't speak that it will. It is just like those HOT pair of shoes that you saw and said to yourself, "Oh next week I'm going to get those." You spoke it and believed it and focused your mind on purchasing those shoes and when the time came you got what you wanted. The new you is so important and you owe it to yourself to speak it, believe it, and become it. Don't allow anyone to silence your voice. Don't except the normal, the status quo or become comfortable in your current state. Speak the word of God and speak what you desire to see and watch it change. I speak to you today that it is time to embrace your freedom of speech. Speak into the atmosphere and call forth everything that belongs to you. You don't have to accept what can be changed. As you walk in your identity and purpose, I encourage you to not only ask for what you desire, but speak it as well. There is power in your words that can transform your life and the world you live in.

Today, I empower you to wake up your voice and speak. Decree, declare, command, believe, and it will be established. Your life will change for the better!

Daily Scripture
"You shall also decide and decree a thing, and it shall be established for you; and the light [of God's favor] shall shine upon your ways."
(Job 22:28AMP)

Prayer
Father, I thank you for the ability to speak. I thank you for being my example of the power of the spoken word. I pray that you will continue to give me visions and dreams so I may speak and watch them come to pass. Thank you for allowing me to bring Glory to your name by speaking your word to cause an impact and change in the lives of others. In Jesus name, Amen.

Reflection
I challenge you to consistently speak what you desire to see. Practice speaking positive words over your life.

Are you willing to make a serious commitment to using the power of the spoken word?

Has disappointment or lack of manifestation hindered your faith in speaking?

Faith Confession
I will awaken my voice and speak change and transformation in my life. I will speak positive affirmations and speak what I expect to see in my future.

DAY 34

Imagine Me – Above and Beyond

It can be dangerous to know how great you are but it is extremely dangerous if you do not know that you are great.

Do you remember hearing the phrase "the sky is the limit" or "reach for the stars"? Those were phrases that motivated me to reach toward my dreams. I thought that having the motivation to be successful and achieve what I knew was attainable was enough. But now later in my life, I realize that I was still limiting myself of what I could really be. Just close your eyes right now and think of that vision of your life with no limits. Think of that dream that you want so bad you can touch it. God has given you that desire, vision, and dream and He wants to do above and beyond what you can imagine or think. How is that possible? Can you even conceive it in your finite mind? But that is the awesome thing about God, He is of infinite wisdom and power and He can do that which seems impossible to man. It is right within your reach but you must expand your mind in order to perceive what it is. He has given you the freedom to be. To be what? To be above and beyond what you are able to comprehend right now. To no longer be on the outside looking in but to be a part of the dream. God wants to stretch your mind and imagination that what was once your ultimate dream becomes small and is replaced with something even greater.

I believe that your territory will be enlarged as soon as your perspective is refined. You will only receive more when the capacity of your mind has been enlarged. Stretch, stretch, stretch, for your greater is coming. Imagine YOU, yes YOU, above and beyond what you could ever dream, think, imagine, or ask.

Today, I challenge you to go beyond the sky and the

stars and dream again. Set your mind to pursue and receive

the unexpected.

Daily Scripture
"Now unto him that is able to do exceedingly abundantly above all that we ask or think, according to the power that worketh in us"
(Ephesians 3:20 KJV)

Prayer
Father I give you praise for thinking of me before the foundations of the world. Thank you for loving me enough to give me your very best. I pray that you would expand my mind that I would come to know just how valuable I am. Allow me to dream new dreams and see new visions. In Jesus name, Amen.

Reflection
Do you believe God can do above what you ask or think?

Are you willing to be stretched to the place of receiving something new?

Identify those things that have become barriers to you imagining and desiring more.

Faith Confession
Today, I open up my mind and heart to dream again. I open up my spirit and relinquish myself to another level of consciousness so I can receive what God has for me.

DAY 35

A Woman of Influence

———————————— ❋ ————————————

You are the blessing. Give of yourself. It is so rewarding.

I believe that discovering and becoming the new you is not just about you, but about what you can offer the world. Oftentimes, we can get so caught up in becoming a better person and creating a better life for ourselves that we forget that we were created to be a blessing. What you are purposed to do will overflow into the world and make an impact in the lives of others. You are a woman of influence. Your gifts and talents are not to be put on the shelf but to influence your family, your children, your co-workers, and our friends. We all have a story and a testimony that is unique, but what good is it if others don't hear it. There are people who need to hear your testimony. It may give someone hope and strength to live again, to not give up, and to believe that better is on the way. It means nothing if you are successful and prosperous, but you fail to make a great impact. It doesn't cost anything to influence the generation that is coming behind you.

When Jesus stepped on the scene, He made an impact, influenced the culture, and left a lasting impression. What impression have you made? What legacy will you leave? When you become the new you, it is your responsibility to show your sister the way.

Today, I challenge you to make an impact so that others' lives are changed. Reach out and help someone else reach a place of discovery and wholeness through the power of God. That single mother who is ready to give up is waiting on you. That young girl who just had an abortion because the father of her child abandoned her is waiting on you. That woman who wants to go back to school but doesn't think she can is waiting on you. Let the new you lead the way.

Daily Scripture
"Then the eleven disciples went to Galilee, to the mountain where Jesus had told them to go. When they saw him, they worshiped him; but some doubted. Then Jesus came to them and said, "All authority in heaven and on earth has been given to me. Therefore go and make disciples of all nations, baptizing them in the name of the Father and of the Son and of the Holy Spirit, and teaching them to obey everything I have commanded you. And surely I am with you always, to the very end of the age."
(Matthew 28:16-20 NIV)

Prayer
Father, I thank you that you called me great and you said greater works will I do. I make a commitment to honor your word by actively working to be a blessing and create change. I pray that you continue to grace me to carry out the calling that you have placed on my life. In Jesus name, Amen.

Reflection
Do you believe that you were created to make an impact in the world?

What do you offer to the world and the body of Christ?

If you desire to see a change in the world we live in, I challenge you to list things that you can do to make a difference and be a woman of influence.

Faith Confession
I believe that I have been called to make a greater impact in the world. I am committed to giving back and helping my brothers and sisters. I will share my testimony in an effort to free someone else.

CELEBRATE YOURSELF!

Congratulations! You have completed week five of your 40 day journey. There is only five days left! You are free to be you so celebrate! You really deserve it. Do something special for yourself and enjoy your freedom. The New You is just around the corner! It's a revolution!

FIVE DAYS OF GRACE

God's grace – His unmerited favor. God's grace – His gift to us. God's grace – that we sometimes take for granted. It is what covers us and allows us to be. Grace is what keeps us when we shouldn't be kept. Where would you be without grace? I want you to take a moment and mediate on how grace has stood strong in your life. Tears just began to flow because I know I don't deserve it. I know that I haven't been that great but, yet, grace has been extended to me. Just think about your life and all the things that you have done. It is hard not to be grateful and thankful for God's gift of grace. It is so precious and valuable.

God spoke to me that this week would be the five days of grace. He has graced you with another chance to get it right, to go beyond the surface, to discover something new, and to be all that you were purposed to be. God has also graced you, equipped you, inspired you, and empowered you to operate in your unique gifting. You are only able to do what you do because He has graced you to do it. That is why you can endure all that you have and juggle three different assignments at the same time, where someone else would have given up. It is all because of grace! He has given you the grace to be. In spite of everything going on around you remember that His grace is sufficient for you. It's like a surfer in the middle of an ocean on his surfboard waiting for that one great wave to ride. The only reason why you are able to keep progressing is because God has allowed you to ride the waves of grace. It is going to sustain you, cover you, and present you polished and refined. This week I want you to focus on the grace of God. This week is about some key elements that are essential in being the new you. You will focus on Strength, Joy,

Clarity, Peace, and Wholeness. These elements may seem simple but they are very powerful.

DAY 36

Strength

You can never use your physical strength to be victorious in a spiritual battle.

"Fear not, for I am with you; be not dismayed, for I am your God; I will strengthen you, I will help you, I will uphold you with my righteous right hand."(Isaiah 41:10)

Are you feeling weary? Do you need refueling? Does it feel as though the weight of it all is resting on your shoulders? I have good news. God has given you strength. Living through a time of transformation and discovery may feel as though you have given all you have. I can testify that you are in the best place for God's strength to be present in your life. When you are weak, then you are strong in Christ. His strength takes over. But I understand that as we weather the storms and move through the obstacles it seems that strength is nowhere to be found. That is when you have to pull on who you are in the spirit and allow it to supersede those disillusioned feelings of weakness. "God has equipped you with strength. He has made your feet like that of a deer and sets you secure on heights."(Psalm 18:32-34) Do you understand how powerful that is? Your strength doesn't run out because you are weak; because that is the time that His strength is made perfect in you. You are more than able to conquer anything that is set before you. Will it be a struggle at times for you to tap into it, yes it will. There will be moments when you may not want to get out of the bed be encouraged that strength will give you momentum to press forward. Your future depends on it.

As you walk in your newness your strength will be tested, but you will come out on top. The more you move in purpose and in timing your strength will be renewed. Isn't it ironic how strength is activated in times of distress? A situation may hit your life that takes your breath away.

Initially you may react through your emotions but all of a sudden you find yourself speaking empowering words and encouraging yourself. Girl, by the end of the day, you are in war mode ready to conquer and defeat. Your strength can't be exercised until you effectively use it in battle. Today, I challenge you to adjust your focus and look for opportunities to increase in strength. You already have the victory, so don't stop short of your promise. Just remember you are strong and you are equipped for it all.

Daily Scripture
"Therefore I take pleasure in infirmities, in reproaches, in necessities, in persecutions, in distresses for Christ's sake: for when I am weak, then am I strong."
(2 Corinthians 12:10 KJV)

Prayer
Father, I thank you for being my strong tower. Thank you for being my refuge and my strength. I pray that you would continue to show yourself strong in my life. I pray that when I am weak that your strength would shine through. I am grateful that I don't have to be strong that all I have to do is cast my cares on you. Continue to teach me how to step aside and let you fight my battles. In Jesus name, Amen.

Reflection

Do you have the superwoman syndrome? If so, what makes you feel like you have to be everything to everyone?

Write down three ways that you have activated your natural strength. Now, write down three ways that you can activate your spiritual strength.

Faith Confession

I understand that sometimes there is no need for me to be so strong. It is okay to let go and let God be strong in my life. I can't do it all. I need God's strength in my life. I will remember that whenever I am weak that is an opportunity for me to be strong in Christ. He is my strength.

DAY 37

Joy

When you embrace it…you will live in it.

"I just want to be happy," is what I often shouted. There were so many things I wanted to accomplish in my life. I had this huge vision of what my life was to be and I was expecting to get to that "happy" place. After enduring the ups and downs of life, I began to think that maybe I needed to redefine the meaning of happiness; that maybe what I coined as true happiness didn't exist.

Are you in search of happiness? I believe that happiness is possible and we all deserve it, but God began to focus my attention on embracing the joy that He has given me. Most times happiness and joy are used interchangeably and viewed as the same thing. I believe there is a difference. Happiness can be based on feelings and outward circumstances and situations. Joy is something solid and constant and is an internal position. As people in your life change, circumstances, and situations, if you are not rooted and grounded in joy, your happiness has the ability to fade. Joy remains constant regardless of the temperature around you. Man cannot give you joy because your joy is through your relationship with God. It is an internal assurance. "You will show me the path of life; in your presence is fullness of joy, at your right hand there are pleasures forevermore."(Psalm 16:11 AMP) Your joy is complete when you have a relationship with God and rest in His presence. Even if your current state in life is not what you would like, if you have joy it will produce happiness. Trials can't shake your joy and disappointment, and rejection can't shake your joy. As you become the new you, you will need to operate in joy as it will preserve your state of being and be a magnate to every good thing that God has designed for your life.

Today, I challenge you to transition from happiness to joy! When you are complete with the joy of the Lord true happiness will come. I encourage you to mediate on the joy that you receive in His presence. Today, you shall have unspeakable joy!

Daily Scripture
"Rejoice in the Lord always. I will say it again: Rejoice!"
(Philippians 4:4 NIV)

Prayer
Father, teach me how to place happiness and joy in its perspective places and not try to receive joy through happiness. Show me how to receive and operate in the joy you have given me. I thank you that your joy is my strength and it is what produces happiness in my life. In Jesus name, Amen.

Reflection
What is your definition of happiness? What is your definition of joy?

What does your vision of true happiness look like?

Do you truly have the joy of the Lord?

What are things you can do to operate in joy?

Faith Confession

I believe that true happiness exists and it is achievable. It is okay to be happy, but I need to find and operate in joy. I will walk in the fullness of joy and let it be my strength.

DAY 38

Clarity

You can't receive manifestation until you receive and understand the full revelation.

The truth hurts however it is necessary for your growth and spiritual maturity. Truth also exposes the enemy and brings forth deliverance. My prayer has always been, "Lord give me clarity." But what I realized is that I was praying that prayer but wasn't truly ready to accept what He revealed. "And ye shall know the truth, and the truth shall make you free."(John 8:22 KJV) When you come into the knowledge of truth, you will be free of the lies of the enemy. Do you desire clarity? Are you in search of truth? Are you ready to receive it when God reveals it? I remember watching a sermon and it was as if God himself was speaking to me. I began to cry and everything hit me all at once. All of the revelations and prophetic words all fit together and made perfect sense. No longer were they independent of each other, for on this day they all came together as one big announcement of clarity and truth. It was as if the scales were removed from my eyes and God clearly showed me how the enemy had been working in my life. It was life-changing for me…my moment of clarity changed my life.

You need a moment of clarity if you are trying to figure out that missing piece in your life. You don't have to stay confused, conflicted, and off-balance. You need God to clearly give you revelation and understanding on the ambiguous areas in your life. You need God to show you the tactic of the enemy so true deliverance and freedom may take place. Clarity is refreshing and it removes the heaviness we often feel when trying to navigate our way through life.

Today, I challenge you to seek the Lord for clarity and be open to receive it when it arrives. You can't be new without allowing God's word to become active in your life. Clarity is no benefit to you if you don't apply what has been revealed.

Daily Scripture
"My son, if you accept my words and store up my commands within you, turning your ear to wisdom and applying your heart to understanding— indeed, if you call out for insight and cry aloud for understanding, and if you look for it as for silver and search for it as for hidden treasure, then you will understand the fear of the LORD and find the knowledge of God. For the LORD gives wisdom; from his mouth come knowledge and understanding."
(Proverbs 2:2-6 NIV)

Prayer
Father, I thank you for the things you are getting ready to reveal to me. I ask for the strength to be strong and receive it with an open heart and apply your word that I can see change in my life. Thank you in advance for revealing the strategies of the enemy that I will be victorious. In Jesus name, Amen.

Reflection
Do you need clarity in your life? In what areas?

Are you ready to receive what God reveals and apply it to your life?

Faith Confession
I am ready for God to reveal to me what I need to know in this season of my life. I will do the necessary work needed to apply the word of God in my life that I become new.

DAY 39

Peace

An inner space that only you and God have access to.

The peace of God is priceless! As women, we juggle so many responsibilities and often give too much of ourselves. We often sacrifice our happiness, joy, and peace for the sake of others. In the midst of our busy lives that we strive to keep in order, it may appear that chaos has taken over and hijacked our peace. Many days I have cried out to the Lord and said, "I just want peace." I would have given anything for peace of mind. I didn't realize that what I was asking for God had already given. "Peace, I leave with you; my peace I give you. I do not give to you as the world gives. Do not let your hearts be troubled and do not be afraid."(John 14:27 NLT) Jesus has already given us the gift of peace. This gift is unlike any other gift that the world gives. This gift doesn't go out of style or depreciate in value over time. This gift is priceless and is an everlasting gift.

Peace is a state of being and you have been given the authority of peace. How is it that Jesus can be in a boat on the sea while the storm is raging and be at peace? All of the disciples are in a panic but Jesus simply says, "peace be still". He commanded the peace that he possessed to take authority over the storm. You may be in a crazy situation right now but you have the authority to command peace to overtake it. No longer will you seek for something that you already have. You don't have to respond in fear or worry when challenging times arise. Just operate in the gift of peace and your response will be that of calmness, confidence, and victory. The next time you find yourself conflicted, I challenge you to tap into the peace of God and let it work on your behalf. Don't allow your finances, spouse, children, lies, job, or anything else rob you of your peace. Some of you may be asking, "How do I operate in the peace of God?" We operate by praying about everything and worrying about nothing. God doesn't desire for us to worry, but to cast our cares on Him and communicate with Him so He can guide our lives. Meditate on God's word and His goodness and allow that to rule your life. You may need to develop strategies when you feel worry, fear, and anxiety creeping in. Begin to recite scriptures, pray, listen to inspirational and worship music, do whatever you need to do to shift yourself into a posture of peace.

Today, let the peace of God go beyond your understanding and govern your heart.

Daily Scripture

Do not be anxious about anything, but in every situation, by prayer and petition, with thanksgiving, present your requests to God. And the peace of God, which transcends all understanding, will guard your hearts and your minds in Christ Jesus. Finally, brothers and sisters, whatever is true, whatever is noble, whatever is right, whatever is pure,

whatever is lovely, whatever is admirable—if anything is
excellent or praiseworthy—think about such things."
(Philippians 4:6-9 NIV)

Prayer
Father, I thank you for being my peace when it seems that
chaos is all around me. Teach me Lord to rest in your peace
when I am unsettled in my spirit. I pray that you give me
the peace that surpasses all understanding. Even when I
don't understand I know that I can find a calm place in you.
I ask that you would allow peace to govern my heart. In
Jesus name, Amen.

Reflection
Do you desire peace in your life?

Are you willing to make the necessary adjustments to clear
the clutter and chaos so peace can abound?

What are some practical things you can do to operate in
peace?

Faith Confession
I decree and declare that I will operate in peace regardless
of what is going on around me. I will no longer allow
people and situations to steal my peace.

DAY 40

Wholeness

It can't be bought. It can't be fabricated. It must be complete in Him.

As I sit to write, I am reminded of a great song by Ledisi entitled "Pieces of Me". It has a great beat and lyrics that women can relate to. I believe we all can agree that there are many pieces to who we are. While it is great to recognize your many facets, it is equally important to be sure they aren't disjointed from each other. Every part of you must fit together and complement each other making you whole. Being whole does not mean that you are defined by one particular attribute. I recently had a revelation that no one word or phrase could define who I was and what I was purposed to do. I see myself as a quilt made up of many different parts and shapes but each one adds value to the next and becomes a key fabric of the essence of me. Being whole is not based on what you have, but it is the result of being complete in Christ. I remember seeking validation, happiness, and fulfillment from relationships, and I would continuously come up empty and unsatisfied. I knew there was a void but, I was trying to fill a spiritual need with a natural solution and that never works. The process to wholeness never involves covering your wounds with band-aids in the form of material possessions and ungodly connections and soul ties.

God wants you to be healthy and whole. He desires for you to experience victory in every area of your life. If you are tired of being empty and unsatisfied you need to let God in and allow Him to transform your life. "Beloved, I pray that you may prosper in every way and [that your body] may keep well, even as [I know] your soul keeps well *and* prospers."(3 John 1:2AMP) God wants you to prosper in every area of your life. He wants you to be healthy and of sound mind. This can't happen unless you are willing to allow God to process you to a place of complete wellness in your spirit, body, and soul. Your spiritual journey is not void of hard work, time, and discipline. A transformed, prosperous, and victorious life means a life of surrender unto God and a commitment to change. Aren't you tired of being hurt and disappointed? Aren't you tired of feeling spiritually and emotionally bankrupt? You deserve to be exactly who God called you to be. It is time for you to disconnect from everything and everyone that interferes with you being whole. No longer will you sacrifice yourself to attempt to save someone else. No longer will you believe the lies of the enemy and accept your current state as your destiny. God wants you to come away with Him and spend intimate time with Him. Only He can heal the broken pieces and make the crooked places straight in your life. You owe it to God and yourself to be an excellent representation of Christ.

Today, I want you to imagine your life once you are whole. I just got excited at the vision I saw! Keep that vision at the forefront of your mind, stay focused, and watch your life change! It is time to be whole and healed. You are worth it!

Daily Scripture
"Have nothing to do with godless myths and old wives' tales; rather, train yourself to be godly. For physical training is of some value, but godliness has value for all things, holding promise for both the present life and the life to come. This is a trustworthy saying that deserves full acceptance."
(1 Timothy4:7-9 NIV)

Prayer
Father, I thank you for provisions that you have given me. I thank you for healing, protection, and prosperity. I am so grateful for being made whole and complete in you. Thank you for loving me. In Jesus name, Amen.

Reflection
Do you desire to be whole? What does being whole look like?

List some things that you can do to assist in you becoming whole and healed.

Faith Confession

I deserve to be whole and healed and not lacking anything.
I am worth it. I will prosper in my health, mind, body, soul,
and spirit. I am complete because of who I am in Christ.

THE NEW YOU!

Congratulations! You have successfully completed your 40 day journey. How do you feel? After I finished, it was bittersweet. I was excited that I completed the journey, but I was looking forward to going further. I wanted to extend it to 60 days, 90 days, or even 120 days! What it did for me was adjust my habits and my lifestyle. So although I am not actually still on my 40 day journey, I am continuing the process of self-examination and increasing my relationship with God. I hope this has also proven to be a lifestyle change for you as well; not just a 40 day challenge or task. You too can continue with growing, evolving, and climbing to new heights of intimacy in your relationship with God. I urge you not to go back to your same routine or cycle that existed before your 40 days. I encourage you to press forward with the same attitude, posture, and mindset that you developed during your journey. The test was not the process of the 40 days, but your test will be in your ability to maintain the new you. Enjoy where you are right now and don't apologize for your newfound focus and confidence. You have now gone through the discovery process and, more than likely, your perspective of everything in your life has changed. Your priorities may be shifting, your relationships may change, and your attitude may seem somewhat selfish. It is okay. It comes along with the new you and so does a little apprehension. Whenever you experience change it may bring some uncertainties along with excitement. You are excited about the new you and what is in store for you, however, you may also feel a bit apprehensive about the unknown. You are in an excellent position for God to work in your life. Are you excited? You can do it! I believe in you. Welcome to the new you!

www.ingramcontent.com/pod-product-compliance
Lightning Source LLC
Chambersburg PA
CBHW051829090426
42736CB00011B/1713